# THE AI ADVANTAGE NOBODY'S TEACHING

*How Solo Operators Are Using Claude to Out-Think, Out-Build, and Out-Execute the Competition*

Kevin Noble

Noble Publishing House

Published by Noble Publishing House

First Edition, 2026

# TABLE OF CONTENTS

*If this book helps you, I'd be genuinely grateful if you took 60 seconds to leave a review on Amazon. Honest reviews from real readers are what help independent authors reach more people. Even a sentence or two makes a real difference.*

*Thank you.*

*-Kevin Noble*

# Introduction

*The Conversation That Needs To Be Had*

Everyone has an opinion about AI right now. Most of those opinions are wrong. Not because people are stupid, but because they have been comparing the wrong things, asking the wrong questions, and measuring results against expectations that were never realistic to begin with.

The conversation goes like this: someone tries ChatGPT, gets something mediocre, and either decides AI is overhyped or decides they just need a better prompt. They Google "how to write better prompts," find some listicle, try again, get something slightly less mediocre, and conclude that this is what AI is. A slightly smarter autocomplete that writes passable emails and generates blog posts nobody wants to read.

The conversation nobody's having is about what happens when you bring something real to the table. When the person sitting across from the AI actually has something at stake, a business to run, a product to launch, a decision to make, a brand to build, and they approach the tool with the same rigor they'd bring to hiring a talented collaborator. What happens then is measurably, practically, obviously different.

I know this because I live it.

> *I'm not a prompt engineer. I'm not an AI researcher. I'm a founder, a producer, a writer, and a person who runs too many things at once. Claude has become the most valuable collaborator in my working life.*

As of this writing, I operate Legends Sauce Co., a specialty hot sauce and condiment brand. Saucestronauts, the story universe and content wing of that same brand. Reserve Labs, a supplement company I'm building in parallel. And Noble Publishing House, the imprint that's publishing this book. I also write political commentary under the pen name Sullivan Knox, produce music, and am somewhere in the middle of building a fictional IP universe called The Republic of Carnivoreland that may or may not have aired its first animated show by the time you read this book.

I do most of this alone, not because I can't hire people (though budget is always a factor in today's society of ever growing labor expenses), but because the kind of work that moves a brand forward requires judgment, voice, and context that's hard to delegate to someone who just showed up and is more or less in this only for a paycheck.

The thinking can't be outsourced. The decisions can't be templated. The voice has to be mine.

What Claude does is compress the distance between the thinking and the doing.

That's the book in one sentence. Everything that follows is an explanation of how, why, and what it looks like in practice.

## WHY THIS BOOK EXISTS

Browse any digital shelf and you'll find no shortage of books about AI productivity. Most of them were written by consultants who want to sell you a course, by tech writers fascinated by the technology but who've never run a business with it, or by prompt engineers who've reverse-engineered some clever tricks but have no real stakes in the outcomes.

They'll teach you to write a decent cold email. They'll show you how to summarize a PDF. They'll give you a hundred prompts for social media captions.

That's fine, and it's not nothing. But it's not this.

This book is written from inside the work. Every technique I describe, I've used under real conditions. The investor letter actually had to land. The brand copy actually had to convert. The production timeline actually had to hold. I'm not showing you what's theoretically possible with AI. I'm showing you what I've actually done with Claude, and how you can build the same kind of working relationship.

There are a lot of Claude books on the market right now, and most of them treat the tool the same way the general conversation treats AI: as a feature to be unlocked, a set of tricks to be memorized, a machine to be optimized. They're not wrong, exactly. But they're missing the thing that actually makes Claude valuable, which isn't the technology. It's the relationship that it has with the user.

Claude rewards someone who can articulate what they actually need. Someone who can hold a real conversation, push back on a weak answer, and build on a strong one. Someone who brings context to the table instead of just requests. That's the person this book is for.

## WHY CLAUDE SPECIFICALLY

You may be thinking, why write a book about Claude and not about AI in general?

Because they're not the same. I've used the major models. I use Claude far and away the most frequently now, and not out of brand loyalty or affiliation. I have none. I use it because of how it thinks and because of how it communicates.

Claude has a longer context window than most competitors, which matters more than people realize. It means you can load a full brand brief, a style guide, a competitive analysis, and a specific ask into the same conversation and have Claude actually hold all of it in mind while it works. That significantly changes what's possible.

Claude reasons differently than your other popular LLMs. Ask it to stress-test a business decision and it'll actually stress-test it, surfacing objections you hadn't considered instead of just validating what you already said like a certain Open AI creation. That distinction matters when you're using an AI for anything beyond content generation.

And Claude writes in a voice that doesn't immediately read as AI-generated. That's harder to achieve than it sounds, and it matters enormously when you're using it for brand copy, investor materials, or any creative work where the output is going to be read by someone who's been trained by the internet to spot the tell-tale signs of machine writing.

None of this is to say Claude is perfect. There's a whole chapter on its limitations, and I mean it. Knowing what to trust and what to verify is as important as knowing how to prompt. But for the kind of work that fills my days, it's the best tool I've found.

## HOW TO READ THIS BOOK

This book is organized in four parts.

Part One is about why Claude is built differently, as a user's-eye-view of what makes it distinct and why that matters in practice. If you've already used Claude extensively, you can skim Part One and jump to Part Two. If you're newer to the tool or coming from heavy ChatGPT use, read it carefully. The mindset shift it's trying to produce is the foundation for everything that follows.

Part Two is the prompt playbook. This is the structural and tactical layer of how to actually get Claude to do its best work. We'll get into the anatomy of a real prompt, the art of the follow-up, and how to build conversations with intent instead of just sending requests into a void.

Part Three is use cases: brand building, operations, creative work, strategic thinking, and writing with a point of view. Each chapter is built around real examples from real work, with enough specificity that you can extract frameworks and apply them to your own situation.

Part Four is about building a sustainable AI workflow. How to make Claude a default part of your daily operations rather than an occasional resource you remember to use when you're stuck.

The Appendix at the back is a prompt library: 50+ copy-paste-ready prompts organized by use case. Use it as a starting kit, not a ceiling.

This book does not require you to be a tech person, nor does it require you to be particularly comfortable with AI, or to have any background in machine learning, or to understand what a large language model is at a mechanistic level. What it does require is that you be someone with real work to do and the willingness to think seriously about how to do it better.

If that's you, keep reading.

*Kevin Noble*

PART ONE: WHY CLAUDE IS BUILT DIFFERENT

# CHAPTER ONE

## The Model They Built for Thinkers

*What Claude actually is, and why it matters to people who do real work*

There is a version of this chapter that reads like a product brochure. It talks about parameter counts and training pipelines and constitutional AI frameworks and transformer architectures. That version exists in a lot of places on the internet. You don't need it here.

What you need is a working understanding of how Claude is different from what you've probably already tried, explained in terms of what that difference actually produces when you sit down to work with it. That's what this chapter is.

We'll talk about the technology, but only as far as it explains the behavior. The goal is to make you a more effective user of how to use AI as a specific tool, starting with understanding why that tool works the way it does.

## THE PROBLEM WITH HOW MOST PEOPLE THINK ABOUT AI

Most people, when they think about AI language models, picture something like a very sophisticated search engine. You put in a question, it retrieves a relevant answer. The better the question, the better the retrieval. This model of thinking produces a certain kind of user behavior: you ask short questions, you evaluate the first response, you either accept it or try a slightly different phrasing, and you repeat until you get something usable.

That behavior makes sense if you're using a search engine. It does not make sense if you're using Claude.

The better mental model is closer to a conversation with a capable analyst who has read an enormous amount, thinks carefully before responding, and gets better the more context you give them. The key word in that sentence is *conversation.* You're not querying. You're not requesting. Don't even think of it as prompting, even though we'll use that word throughout this book because it's become the industry standard. Think **conversation.**

That distinction shapes everything that follows in this book, and it starts with understanding what Claude actually is under the hood.

## WHAT CLAUDE IS, IN PLAIN TERMS

Claude is a large language model built by Anthropic, a company founded in 2021 by former members of OpenAI, including Dario Amodei and Daniela Amodei. Anthropic's founding thesis was that building AI safely and building AI well were not competing goals, but complementary ones. That thesis has shaped the way Claude was trained.

At the technical level, Claude is trained on a large corpus of text from the internet, books, and other sources, and it learns to predict what comes next in a sequence of words. That's true of all large language models, including whatever iteration of ChatGPT and Gemini we're currently on at your time of reading this. The interesting differences are in what happens on top of the basic mechanisms of each.

Anthropic developed an approach called Constitutional AI, which is a method for training models to be helpful, harmless, and honest by having the model evaluate and critique its own outputs against a set of principles during training. The result is a model that has, for lack of a better word, internalized certain values about how to communicate, when to push back, and how to handle ambiguity.

You feel this in practice before you understand it technically. Claude will tell you when it thinks your premise is wrong. It will flag uncertainty instead of papering over it with confident-sounding nonsense. It will ask for clarification on an ambiguous request rather than guessing and producing something that misses the point. These are characteristics baked into how the model thinks.

> *Most AI tools are built to make you feel like the interaction worked. Claude is built to make the interaction actually work. That's a different design goal, and it produces a different product.*

## THE CONTEXT WINDOW: WHY IT CHANGES EVERYTHING

If there's one technical concept worth understanding deeply before you start working with Claude, it's the context window.

The context window is the amount of text Claude can hold in active consideration during a conversation. Think of it as working memory. Everything you've written, everything Claude has responded, every document you've pasted in, every instruction you've given: all of it lives in the context window. When the context window fills up, older content starts to fall out of active consideration.

Claude's context window is large, substantially more so than most competing models at most price points. The current versions support hundreds of thousands of tokens, which translates to roughly hundreds of pages of text that Claude can actively reason about at once.

Most of the genuinely useful things you want to do with an AI require holding a lot of information at the same time. You want Claude to write investor materials that are consistent with your brand voice, grounded in your actual business model, and targeted at a specific kind of investor. That means Claude needs to have your brand voice guide, your business overview, your financial snapshot, and your target investor profile all in mind simultaneously while it writes.

With a smaller context window, you're making tradeoffs constantly. You're deciding which information to include and which to leave out, knowing that whatever you leave out won't be reflected in the output. With a large context window, you can just include everything. You stop making tradeoffs and start having real conversations.

I've loaded entire brand bibles into a Claude session and then spent an hour working through copy, positioning, and strategy, with Claude holding the full context of the brand throughout. The outputs are categorically different from what you get when you're working piecemeal, feeding Claude one fragment of context at a time and hoping it remembers what you told it three prompts ago. It doesn't have to remember. It can see it all.

## REASONING VS. PREDICTING

Here is the claim that will sound most like marketing until you experience it firsthand: Claude does more than just predict. It actually reasons.

Every large language model is, at the mathematical level, doing next-token prediction, Claude included. So when I say Claude reasons, I don't mean it's doing something mechanically different from other models. I mean that the training, the scale, and the architecture have produced a model whose outputs are consistent with what we'd call reasoning if a person produced them.

What does that look like in practice? You describe a business problem, and instead of getting back a generic list of solutions scraped from the internet, you get a response that identifies the specific tension in your situation, names the tradeoffs, offers a recommendation with a stated rationale, and flags the assumptions it's making. You can then push back on those assumptions, and Claude will actually engage with your pushback instead of just restating its original answer.

Most software cannot change its mind when challenged because it has no mind to change. Claude can. And once you've tasted that, returning to the others feels like stepping out of a Michael Mann thriller and back into a Saturday morning cartoon.

## THE VOICE QUESTION

Then there is the dimension that matters most for those of us who traffic in words: Claude can *write.*

It writes with rhythm, with subordination, with a point of view that doesn't collapse into either pomposity or pandering. It can sound like authority without wearing a suit. It can sound like you—your cadences, your characteristic moves, your particular flavor of savagery—once you've given it enough examples to study.

This is no accident of scale, but instead the residue of training on oceans of serious human prose. The model didn't just learn language. It learned *style*. And when you know how to feed it, it becomes the most dangerous writing collaborator alive.

This is the capability that I've found most valuable and most underutilized so we'll spend a full chapter on this later. For now, the point is that this capability exists and that it comes from something real in how the model was trained, and that shows up when you give it the right inputs.

## WHAT THIS MEANS FOR YOU

Here's the practical upshot of everything in this chapter: Claude is not a better search engine. It is not a faster way to find information you could find yourself. If that's how you're using it, you are committing a quiet form of intellectual self-harm

It is a thinking partner. A mind that rewards complexity, specificity, and judgment. It is most valuable precisely when the problem is hard, the context is rich, and the stakes require something more than retrieval. Treat it like a capable collaborator you have just briefed on the full dossier and less like a carnival machine you're shaking for better prizes, and it will repay you in ways few tools ever have.

That mental model shift is the real prerequisite. Everything else in this book—prompting strategies, workflows, advanced applications—rests upon it.

If something isn't working as well as you hoped, return to this chapter. The failure is rarely in the prompt. It is almost always in the way you're still thinking about the machine.

# CHAPTER TWO

## The Operator Mindset

*Why most people stay stranded at the surface, and how the serious ones learn to dive*

There is a word the technologists love to throw around: "operator." In their world it means the sharp-elbowed builder who takes a raw model and bends it to his will: configuring, constraining, ruling the environment. I'm stealing the term for something more useful.

I want it to describe *you*, the individual who refuses to treat Claude like a slightly brighter search bar and instead learns to command it like a loaded weapon.

Most users remain requesters. They type a wish, receive a reply, shrug if it's mediocre, tweak the wording, and repeat until something usable falls out. Transactional. Shallow. Safe.

Operators do something far more dangerous. They *set the arena* before the fight begins. That single distinction—requester versus operator—explains why some people get revolutionary work out of Claude and why most get polite, forgettable competence. Everything that follows in this book flows from it.

## WHAT REQUESTERS DO

Watch a requester in the wild. He needs copy for a new hot sauce. He or she types: *Write a product description for a small-batch habanero hot sauce.*

Claude obliges. It deploys the usual suspects—"bold," "complex," "artisanal"—throws in a limp call-to-action, and sounds exactly like every other craft condiment on the internet. Because that is precisely what it was trained to imitate.

The requester frowns, then tries again: *Make it more exciting.*

Now we get exclamation points and stronger adjectives. Still generic. Just louder. A few more half-hearted passes, a tolerable compromise is reached, and the file is closed. Usable. Never excellent. Never truly their own.

This is the ceiling for requesters. They are playing three-card monte against a house that has already palmed the queen and simply write-off the game as unwinnable.

## WHAT OPERATORS DO

An operator with the same task begins long before the actual request. He understands that Claude is not psychic. It is extraordinarily capable, but it knows nothing about *his* sauce, *her* brand, *his* customers, or *her* particular flavor of savagery unless it's told.

So we brief it first.

We pour in the brand's soul: what it stands for, who actually buys it and why, the origin story that isn't marketing theater, how this sauce fits into the larger line, the exact tone of voice the brand uses in the wild, the words it would rather die than utter, and the verifiable differences that separate it from the vinegar forward sea of imitators.

All of this can be raw, fragmented, conversational. The point is to give Claude the full dossier instead of a Post-it note.

Only then does the operator make the request.

What returns is no longer interchangeable commodity copy but something that carries the brand's fingerprint. It deploys specific, earned details. It possesses a point of view. It could not have been written for any other hot sauce on earth, because the machine was operating on *intelligence* instead of taking shots in the dark.

> *The output is only as specific as the input. Vague prompts produce vague results not because Claude is lazy, but because Claude is doing exactly what you asked: filling in the gaps with whatever seemed most plausible. Give it fewer gaps to fill.*

That's the operator in action. And once you've built the habit, it's actually faster, because you stop cycling through iterations trying to coax something specific out of a tool you gave nothing specific to work with.

## BRIEFING CLAUDE LIKE A COLLABORATOR

Picture this: you have just hired a brilliant, slightly dangerous strategist who has read every important document produced in the last 50 years but knows absolutely nothing about *your* operation.

You could toss him a task cold and receive something competent. Or you could spend half an hour bringing him fully into the conspiracy—context, history, objectives, landmines—and watch everything he touches thereafter become sharper, more precise, more lethal.

Claude is that strategist. The briefing *is* the work.

## THE THREE THINGS OPERATORS ALWAYS BRING

Across thousands of sessions, the pattern becomes unmistakable. The best operators reliably deliver three elements, whether they're building a brand manifesto or dissecting a balance sheet.

**Context.** Who you are. What you're building. The relevant slice of reality that matters for this task. Not your autobiography, just the intelligence the model needs to stop hallucinating in the dark.

**Constraints.** Hard boundaries. Word count. Forbidden phrases. Shelf-life realities. Regulatory tripwires. Audience attention span measured in seconds, not hours. Claude optimizes ruthlessly for whatever you declare non-negotiable. Give it nothing and it will optimize for generic applause.

**Intent.** Not merely what you want written, but what you are actually trying to *accomplish* in the world. A vendor email is one thing. A vendor email designed to renegotiate pricing on a critical run without torching a two-year relationship is something else entirely. Claude needs to feel the difference.

Context. Constraints. Intent. Master these three and you will outperform every prompt-engineering gimmick on the market.

## SESSIONS VS. SINGLE PROMPTS

The requester's delusion is that salvation lies in the Perfect Prompt—a single, hermetically sealed incantation that will deliver glory in one shot. When it inevitably falls short, they are lost. *OMG, the sacred prompt has failed. Now what?*

Operators think in *sessions*, creating living conversations with shape, memory, and direction.

A session has a beginning (the briefing), a middle (the work, the critique, the refinement, the pushback), and an end (an output that has been stress-tested in real time). Inside that session you can do what no single prompt allows: ask Claude to tear apart its own last output, redirect without losing prior intelligence, explain its reasoning, or fix only the paragraph that's bleeding while leaving the rest intact.

This is collaboration, not automation. A vending machine dispenses whereas a worthy partner *develops*, building on what came before.

## BUILDING THE HABIT

The operator mindset is not complex, but it does require a deliberate break from muscle memory.

Before you type your first real request in any new session, pause. Ask yourself: *What would a first-rate collaborator need to know to do this properly?* Dump that information in first even if it's rough or feels inefficient. Then issue the order.

Do this religiously for two weeks and the transformation will embarrass you because you finally stopped treating it like a slightly better autocomplete and started treating it like what it is: a mind waiting for marching orders.

The rest of this book is written for people who have made that shift. Part Two shows you exactly how to structure the intelligence you bring. Part Three catalogs what operators in different domains—branding, operations, creative warfare, strategic thinking—actually feed the machine and what they receive in return.

All of it rests on one foundational truth: you are briefing a collaborator, not submitting a form.

It may seem like a more difficult task yet it is also an infinitely more interesting one.

# CHAPTER THREE

## Context Is Everything

*And most people are still feeding the machine table scraps*

If you carry only one commandment out of this entire section and brand it onto your forehead, let it be this: **load the context before you make the request.**

It sounds almost insultingly simple because it is simple. It is also the difference between people who extract genuine gold from Claude and those who spend their days in an endless, soul-crushing loop of mediocre prompts and polite garbage outputs.

We touched on the technical majesty of the context window in Chapter One. This chapter is about what you actually *do* with that power before the machine even begins its work, how to think about what belongs in the session, how to structure it so Claude doesn't have to guess, and how to stop mistaking a context failure for a prompting failure.

### THE GAP CLAUDE IS ALWAYS TRYING TO FILL

Every time you speak to Claude, it is balancing on a knife's edge between two realities: what you bothered to tell it, and the vast statistical ocean it swallowed during training.

When your input is thin, it leans harder on the ocean, and the ocean, by its nature, is general. It knows every hot sauce that ever existed on the internet. It does not know *yours*. So it does what any well-trained courtier does: it fills the void with the most plausible, most average, most forgettable version of reality.

The result is competent. Interchangeable. The literary equivalent of a McMansion in a subdivision—perfectly fine for someone else.

Context is how you close that gap. It is the difference between "build me a house" and "build me the house that makes sense on *this* awkward lot, under *these* HOA restrictions, for *these* specific people who hate open-concept kitchens and love morning light in the study."

Without context, Claude is simply being exactly as generic as you secretly invited it to be. Context is how you get from a house to *your* house. It's how you close the gap between what Claude knows from training and what Claude needs to know to do this specific job well.

## WHAT CONTEXT ACTUALLY INCLUDES

Context is not a polite backstory paragraph. It is four hard layers, and the operators who get lethal results deliver all four.

**First: Situational context.** Who you are, what you're building, and what is actually at stake. Not "I run a food business." Try: "I run a small-batch hot sauce company that moves through specialty grocers and direct-to-consumer buyers who fetishize provenance and craftsmanship the way sneakerheads fetishize limited-drop kicks."

**Second: Audience context.** Who the hell is this for, and what do they actually care about? This is the layer most amateurs murder by omission. Copy for a jaded specialty retail buyer should taste nothing like copy for a wide-eyed Instagram first-timer. Claude can calibrate with surgical precision, but only if you tell it which target is in the crosshairs.

**Third: Constraint context.** These are the steel bars inside which creativity must dance. Word count. Forbidden language. Shelf realities. Regulatory landmines. Platform quirks. A jazz solo inside a strict chord progression is not restricted; it is liberated. Remove the bars and you get noise.

**Fourth: Intent context.** Not what you want written, but what you are trying to *achieve* in the real world. A product description is output. Securing a sample request from a skeptical buyer who already carries three national brands is intent. An email is output. Reopening a relationship with a lapsed account without looking desperate is intent.

Give Claude the *why* and watch it start making choices worthy of a mind instead of a mimic.

> *Most people give Claude the what. The operators who get the best results also give it the why, the who, and the within-what. Those three additions change everything.*

## HOW TO LOAD A SESSION

There is no sacred format. Some operators drop dense paragraphs. Others use bullet-point dossiers. Still others begin with the conversational gut-punch:

"Alright, here's the full conspiracy before we start writing."

The only rule that matters is that if a sharp, capable stranger read only what you just fed Claude, could they do the job well? If the answer is no, you are not finished loading.

Here's what a thin context load looks like compared to a full one, using a real type of task: writing a pitch email to a potential wholesale account.

THIN CONTEXT LOAD:

```
I need a pitch email to a specialty
grocery store buyer for my hot sauce
brand.
```

That's a request, not a context load. Claude will produce something from it. It will hit the expected beats of a pitch email: introduce the product, mention some selling points, suggest a next step. It will be indistinguishable from the pitch email of every other lesser brand.

FULL CONTEXT LOAD:

```
I'm writing a pitch email to the
buyer at a specialty grocery store.
```

Here's what you need to know before we write it.

My brand is [BRAND NAME]. We make small-batch hot sauces using whole ingredients, no fillers or stabilizers. Our flagship sauce uses [KEY INGREDIENT] sourced from [ORIGIN]. We've been operating for [X] years and are currently in [X] doors across [REGION].

The store I'm pitching is [STORE NAME]. It's a single-location independent with a strong focus on local and regional producers. Their current hot sauce set has two or three national brands and a gap in the premium craft segment, which is where we sit.

The buyer's name is [NAME]. I've never met them. I got the contact from another brand they carry.

My goal is not to close a deal in this email. My goal is to get a sample request or a meeting. The tone should be confident but not

```
pushy. I don't want to sound like a
mass pitch. It should feel like I
did my homework on their store
specifically.

Keep it under 200 words. No bullet
points. Don't start with 'I hope
this email finds you well.'
```

Same task. Different inputs. The second version gives Claude a specific brand, a specific store, a specific buyer relationship, a specific goal, a tone requirement, and several constraints. What it produces will be in a different category from what the first version produces.

The second version took maybe three minutes to write. Those three minutes buy you work that doesn't need five humiliating revision rounds.

## THE BRAND BRIEF: YOUR MOST REUSABLE CONTEXT ASSET

If you run a business with a consistent brand identity, the single highest-leverage thing you can build for your Claude workflow is a brand brief.

A brand brief is a document, or a text block, that captures everything Claude needs to know about your brand before doing any work related to it. Done well, you can paste it into the top of any session where you're doing brand work and immediately have a Claude that knows your brand deeply enough to produce outputs that are on-voice, on-message, and brand-consistent.

Keep it ruthless and specific: origin story with teeth, customer psychology, voice (what you sound like *and* what you would never sound like), forbidden phrases, genuine differentiators, current priorities. 300 to 600 words is plenty if every sentence is earned.

Then open every relevant session with: “Here is the brand brief for [NAME]. Hold every detail in mind for the entire conversation.” Paste. Proceed. The difference is that between a ghostwriter and a co-conspirator.

## RECOGNIZING A CONTEXT PROBLEM

Most users get a weak output and immediately assume the prompt needs tweaking. They are usually wrong.

When the result feels generic, off-voice, or strangely purposeless, run the diagnostic first:

- Did I tell Claude exactly who this is for?
- Did I tell it what I'm actually trying to accomplish in the world?
- Did I give it any real constraints?
- Did I give it anything that couldn't apply to a thousand competitors?

If the answer to any of those is "no," stop rephrasing. Feed it context.

Even in long sessions, drift happens. The fix is simple and brutal: re-anchor. "Remember we're writing for [AUDIENCE] in [BRAND VOICE], and the real goal is [INTENT]." 10 seconds. Session saved.

## CONTEXT AS A PRACTICE

Loading context well is a muscle. The first dozen times it will feel slow and slightly ridiculous. You'll worry you're overdoing it, but you almost certainly aren't.

Over time, it becomes fast. You develop a feel for the relevant layers of context for different types of tasks. You build reusable assets like brand briefs that you can drop in without writing from scratch. You get quicker at identifying the audience, the intent, and the constraints for any given piece of work.

And the outputs improve in a way that compounds because you start to build a body of Claude-assisted work that is genuinely consistent with your brand, your voice, and your standards. That consistency is worth something. It's worth a lot, actually, if you're building something that needs to hold together across dozens or hundreds of pieces of content over months and years.

Context is the foundation. Everything we build in the chapters that follow is built on top of it.

# CHAPTER FOUR

## Anatomy of a Prompt That Actually Works

*What goes in, why it matters, and the quiet bloodbath that follows when any piece is missing*

Part One was diagnosis—the uncomfortable mirror held up to how most people still treat Claude like a slightly brighter Magic 8-Ball.

Part Two is the scalpel.

The operator mindset tells you *how* to think. The context framework tells you *what* to bring. This chapter dissects the actual weapon: the prompt itself, its anatomy, its architecture, and the multitude of reasons why most prompts collapse into mediocrity while a structured few cut straight to the bone.

There are no magic phrases here. No enchanted incantations. Only structure—cold, ruthless, and devastatingly effective.

### WHY STRUCTURE MATTERS

Leave a prompt unstructured and you are quietly delegating a dozen critical decisions to a machine that will make them based on statistical averages instead of your actual needs. Decisions about who the output is for, what format it should take, what tone it should use, how long it should be, what it should prioritize, what it should avoid.

A structured prompt eliminates most of that gap before it forms. When you tell Claude who the audience is, it doesn't have to guess. When you specify the format, it doesn't have to choose. When you define the constraints, it doesn't have to infer. A directed Claude produces directed output.

The six components below are the anatomy of a prompt that works. A quick, simple task might only need three or four. But knowing all six, and knowing what each one does, gives you the ability to diagnose any prompt that isn't working and add exactly what it's missing.

## THE SIX COMPONENTS

### 1. Role

*Who Claude should be in this conversation*

Tell the model which blade of its intellect to unsheathe. Not the vague "you are an expert," but "you are a battle-hardened direct-response copywriter who has made specialty food brands infamous from coast to coast."

Role focuses the model. It gives permission. Want brutal honesty on a half-baked business idea? Assign the role of skeptical venture capitalist who has watched three dozen similar concepts flame out in spectacular fashion. The right role transforms polite agreement into something far more useful: intellectual combat.

Telling it to act as a skeptical investor will produce a more useful stress-test than just asking Claude to find problems with your plan. The role gives Claude permission to be direct in a way that a generic request does not.

### 2. Context

*What Claude needs to know before it starts*

We covered this in depth in Chapter Three, so we won't repeat it all here. The short version: context is the situational, audience, constraint, and intent information that tells Claude what it's working with and what the output needs to accomplish.

In the anatomy of a prompt, context typically comes right after the role, before the task. You're establishing the environment before you ask Claude to work in it.

Think of it as briefing a consigliere before he walks into the meeting. Leave him blind and you get generic counsel. Arm him properly and the opposition never sees the knife coming.

### 3. Task

*What you actually want Claude to produce*

Most amateurs begin here which is why most output is landfill.

The task should name the deliverable with cruel specificity. Instead of "help with the launch," prompt "write a 300-word announcement email for the product launch." Swap "ideas for content" with "draft the opening move in a price renegotiation with a manufacturer we've used for two years."

Specificity is the mold that turns molten talent into a blade.

### 4. Format

*What the output should look like*

Left to its own devices, Claude defaults to the safe, structured, slightly corporate shape it has seen most often. Sometimes that suffices, but more often, it produces visual diarrhea on a product page or a speech that reads like a PowerPoint.

Tell it exactly: under 150 characters, no emojis, no exclamation points or pesky em dashes, short sentences suitable for speaking aloud, clean hierarchy for a one-pager. Tone register (warm, icy, conspiratorial, authoritative) belongs here too. Format is stage lighting, and, if set up wrong, makes even brilliant writing look like amateur theater.

### 5. Constraints

*What the output must not do, and what it must stay within*

Constraints are the boundaries that make good work possible. We covered this in the context chapter, but in the anatomy of a prompt, constraints deserve their own named slot because they are so consistently underprovided.

Constraints include, but are not limited to: word or character limits. Phrases or claims to avoid. Topics that are off-limits. Regulatory or legal requirements. Platform requirements. Things your brand would never say. Things your audience would react negatively to. Prior versions of something you are trying to improve upon and what specifically didn't work about them.

That last one is particularly powerful and almost never used. If you've already tried something and it failed in a specific way, telling Claude what failed and why gives it information that fundamentally changes its approach. Telling it what not to repeat is an entirely different instruction and it produces entirely different results.

### 6. Examples

*What good looks like, in concrete terms*

This is the highest-leverage component most users ignore. Show Claude what victory looks like. Show it what failure tastes like. A single paragraph in the exact voice you want, or a crisp description of tone and temperature, collapses interpretive fog instantly.

The act of providing an example signals to Claude that you have a specific standard in mind. That signal alone changes how carefully it works.

## PUTTING IT TOGETHER: BEFORE AND AFTER

Here is what a prompt looks like when none of these components are present, and what it looks like when all of them are. The task in both cases is the same: writing a social media post for a product launch.

WITHOUT STRUCTURE:

```
Write a social media post for our
new hot sauce launch.
```

Claude will produce something from this that will be vaguely enthusiastic, probably use a fire emoji, mention something about heat or flavor, and end with a few hashtag suggestions. It is the social media post equivalent of the generic contractor's house. Usable, and it comes with furniture, but certainly not *yours*.

WITH STRUCTURE:

```
Role: You are a brand copywriter who
specializes in craft food brands
with cult followings. You write with
personality and restraint. You never
use hype language.


Context: The brand is [BRAND NAME],
a small-batch hot sauce company. Our
voice is confident and dry, never
shouting. Our customer is a
```

food-literate adult who is skeptical of marketing and responds to specificity and honesty. We are launching [PRODUCT NAME], which is made with [KEY INGREDIENT] sourced from [ORIGIN]. This is a limited run of [X] bottles.

Task: Write a single Instagram post announcing the launch.

Format: Under 150 characters. No emojis. No exclamation points. Write it like you're telling a friend about something worth knowing, not advertising to a stranger.

Constraints: Do not use the words 'craft,' 'artisan,' 'small-batch,' or 'fiery.' Do not mention the Scoville scale. Do not include a call to action with a URL.

Example of the right tone: 'Aged six months. Made with one ingredient. This is the vinegar sauce.' That's the level of restraint and specificity we're going for.

What comes back from the second prompt is a different category of output because Claude understood what it was building, for whom, and to what standard.

The second prompt took perhaps four minutes to write. If the first prompt requires multiple rounds of revision to get to something usable, and each round takes two minutes, you've already spent more time on the bad path than the good one would have taken. And the output at the end of the bad path still won't be as good.

## THE MOST COMMON MISTAKE

After working through hundreds of prompting sessions, I've come to believe that the single most common mistake people make is asking for a result instead of setting up a problem.

Asking for a result sounds like: *write me a tagline. Give me ten ideas for content. Draft a response to this email.*

Setting up a problem sounds like: *here is the brand, here is the audience, here is what we've tried before and why it didn't land, here is what we're trying to accomplish, here is what the constraints are. Now: write me a tagline.*

This method gives Claude the material to actually solve it. Asking for a result gives Claude permission to guess.

> *A well-structured prompt is not a longer prompt. It is a complete prompt. The goal is not to write more words. The goal is to leave fewer decisions to chance.*

That distinction matters because the solution is not to make your prompts longer for the sake of length but instead to make them complete. A 40-word prompt that includes role, context, task, format, constraints, and an example will outperform a 200-word prompt that is all task and no structure. Completeness is the variable that keeps our sword sharp and ready for battle.

## WHEN TO USE ALL SIX AND WHEN TO USE FEWER

Not every exchange demands the full ritual. Once rich context is already loaded in an active session, you can fire off surgical two-sentence follow-ups. But when the stakes are real—first drafts, high-visibility work, anything meant to represent you in the world—go deep on all six.

Use the framework as your post-mortem. Output feels off? Run the checklist. The missing or anemic component is almost always the culprit.

Master structure, and Claude stops feeling like a clever toy and starts operating like a co-conspirator who actually understands the mission.

Miss it, and you will keep receiving exactly what you secretly deserve: polite, generic, perfectly average work.

The machine is capable of more.

The question is whether you are.

PART TWO: THE PROMPT PLAYBOOK

# CHAPTER FIVE

## The Conversations That Built Things

*A behind-the-scenes look at real Claude sessions and what came out of them*

Everything before this chapter was necessary scaffolding, but scaffolding never won a war.

This chapter is the war room. Four actual operations, pulled from the trenches of real business work: an investor letter of intent, a content strategy framework, a vendor negotiation email, and a brand voice guide. Not templates for you to Xerox. Templates are for requesters. These are autopsies, not templates for you to Xerox because templates are for requesters. Let's look at exactly how the blood flows when an operator runs a session from setup to lethal finish.

Pay attention to the pattern, because once you see it, you'll recognize it in your own work like a fingerprint at a crime scene.

A note on the examples: the prompts shown here are representative of the type of session described, with details adjusted to be instructive rather than verbatim transcripts. Your own sessions will look different because your situation is different. That's the point.

## WHAT THESE SESSIONS HAVE IN COMMON

Before we get into the individual walkthroughs, it's worth naming the structural pattern that shows up in all four. Every productive Claude session I've run follows roughly the same arc, regardless of the task.

It starts with a setup phase where I load the relevant context and orient Claude to the work. This is usually one substantial message, sometimes two. I'm not making a request yet. I'm building the environment.

Then comes the first output phase, where I make the initial request and Claude produces a first draft or first version. I read it not as a finished product but as a starting point that reveals what Claude understood and what it missed.

Then comes the refinement phase, which is usually two to four exchanges. I'm redirecting, adding information Claude turned out to need, adjusting the scope or tone, pushing back on specific choices. Each exchange produces something closer to the target.

Then comes the extraction phase: taking the final output and putting it where it belongs, whether that's a document, an email, a brand guide, or wherever the work actually lives.

Setup. First output. Refinement. Extraction. That is the operator's dance.

## SESSION ONE: THE INVESTOR LETTER OF INTENT

The scenario: you need to write a letter of intent to a potential investor. One shot at opening a serious conversation with someone who doesn't suffer fools. Something that opens the door, establishes credibility, and gives the recipient a clear reason to respond.

This is a task where the stakes are high, the format is specific, and the voice matters enormously. A letter of intent that sounds like it was generated by AI is a letter of intent that gets kicked to the Archive folder. The task requires the operator approach at its fullest.

### The Setup

---

You begin by painting the full picture, not with a request but with a briefing memo disguised as conversation:

OPENING CONTEXT LOAD:

Before we write anything, I want to give you the full picture.

I'm writing a letter of intent to a potential investor. Here's what you need to know:

About me: I'm the founder of [BRAND], a [CATEGORY] company. I've been operating for [X] years. Current annual revenue is approximately [X]. We're in [X] retail doors and doing [X] in direct-to-consumer. I'm also building [SECOND BRAND] in parallel, which is in [STAGE].

About the investor: [NAME/FIRM] invests in [CATEGORY] consumer brands at the [STAGE] stage. They've backed [COMPARABLE COMPANIES]. I was introduced through [MUTUAL CONNECTION].

What I'm asking for: I'm not asking for a meeting yet. I'm asking for a conversation. I want this letter to establish that I'm building

```
something real, that I understand my
category, and that I'm worth thirty
minutes of their time.


Tone: Direct and confident. Not
pitchy. Not desperate. Write it like
a founder who doesn't need this
particular investor but would be
glad to have them.


Constraints: Under 300 words. No
bullet points. No subject line yet.
First person throughout. Don't start
with 'I hope this finds you well' or
any variation.
```

## The First Output and What It Reveals

Claude produces a first draft. It's good. The structure is right, the tone is close, the length is appropriate. But reading it carefully, two things stand out: it's slightly more formal than the voice you want, and one paragraph leans on generic language about the category rather than the specific details you gave it.

This is normal. The first output tells you what Claude understood and where it made assumptions. The assumption about formality level is easy to correct. The generic paragraph is a context gap. Claude defaulted to category language because the specific information wasn't prominent enough in the setup. You strike back:

REFINEMENT PROMPT:

```
This is close. Two adjustments:

First, pull the formality down about 20%. The current version reads like a business letter. I want it to read like a message from one serious person to another. Less structure, more directness.

Second, the second paragraph is too generic. Replace it with something specific to what makes [BRAND] different in the category. The specific differentiator is [CONCRETE DETAIL]. That detail should be in the letter.
```

The second version is substantially better. One more pass, usually focused on the opening line and the close, and the letter is done.

Total session time: about 25 minutes, or slightly longer than an episode of *Seinfeld*. What you'd have spent writing this from scratch with no AI: at least the length of a Christopher Nolan *Batman* film, and the first draft would still have needed enough editing to get you partially through the sequel.

## SESSION TWO: THE CONTENT STRATEGY

The scenario: you need a content strategy for a brand's social media and email channels. Not a content calendar with specific post ideas, though that will come later. A strategic framework that knows what themes to build around, what formats to use, how to think about the mix of content types across channels.

This is a task where the first instinct, for most people, is to ask Claude to generate ideas. That instinct produces a list of generic content ideas that could apply to any brand in any category. The operator approach starts differently.

### The Setup

---

OPENING CONTEXT LOAD:

I need to build a content strategy for [BRAND]. Before we generate anything, I want to make sure you understand the brand and the business context.

[PASTE BRAND BRIEF HERE]

Business context: We're at a stage where brand awareness is the primary goal. We're not optimizing for conversion yet. We want people who don't know us to encounter the brand and feel something specific: that this is a brand made by someone who actually knows and cares about [CATEGORY].

Channels: Instagram is primary. Email list is secondary, currently [X] subscribers. We post [CURRENT FREQUENCY] and get [ROUGH ENGAGEMENT LEVEL] engagement.

What I need from this session: A strategic framework I can hand to someone and say 'this is how we think about content.' Not a list of post ideas. A framework. Themes,

```
content types, the ratio between
them, and the reasoning behind the
choices.
```

## How the Session Evolves

Claude produces a strategic framework. It's organized around three or four content themes, with a suggested distribution across post types and a brief rationale for each choice. It's solid, like the Robert Pattinson *Batman* movie.

Now the session shifts. Instead of accepting the framework as-is, you push on it. This is where the operator earns the output.

PUSHING DEEPER:

```
The themes make sense. I want to
challenge the third one. You've
suggested [THEME]. My concern is
that this category is already
saturated with that type of content.
Every brand in this space does the
'process and craft' story. What's
the version of that theme that
doesn't look like everyone else?
```

This kind of push produces a materially different response from Claude than a simple revision request would. You're asking it to think harder, not just issue a rewrite. And it does. The response will usually surface a more specific angle, a contrarian take, or a framing that distinguishes your approach from the category default.

One or two exchanges like this, and you have a content strategy that reflects actual thinking about your brand's position, not a generic framework that could belong to any brand in the category.

## SESSION THREE: THE VENDOR NEGOTIATION EMAIL

The scenario: you need to renegotiate pricing with a contract manufacturer you've worked with for two years. The relationship is good, so you don't want to damage it. But your margins are getting compressed—sigh—and you need a better number. The email has to accomplish something specific: open the negotiation without signaling desperation, giving away leverage, or coming across as transactional after fostering a relationship you actually care about.

This is the kind of task where the intent context matters most. The output is an email. But the real task is managing a relationship while pursuing an economic outcome. Those two things are in tension, and Claude needs to understand that tension to write something useful.

OPENING CONTEXT LOAD:

```
I need to write an email to my contract manufacturer to open a conversation about pricing. Here's the full context.

The relationship: We've worked together for two years. The relationship is genuinely good. They've been flexible with us during low-volume periods and we've always paid on time. I consider [CONTACT NAME] a real professional relationship, not just a vendor.

The business situation: Our input costs have increased and our margins are under pressure. I need to bring the per-unit cost down by approximately [X]% to protect the margin at our current price point. I have not yet explored other manufacturers, though I could.
```

```
What I want this email to do: Open the conversation. Not close it. I want them to come back to me with a willingness to talk, ideally with some movement on price or terms. I do not want to issue an ultimatum. I do not want to seem like I'm threatening to leave. I also don't want to undersell the ask.

Tone: Collegial. Direct about the business reality without being clinical. Acknowledge the relationship before getting into the ask.
```

What Claude produces from this setup is an email that does several things at once: acknowledges the relationship, frames the business context as shared rather than adversarial, makes the ask clearly without weaponizing it, and leaves the door open for a conversation rather than demanding a specific outcome.

The refinement pass on this type of email is usually focused on a single line or two: the transition from relationship acknowledgment to the ask is the hinge of the email, and it's worth spending a prompt or two getting that hinge exactly right.

> *The sessions that produce the most useful outputs are usually the ones where the emotional and relational context is as carefully specified as the business context. Claude handles nuance well when you give it nuance to work with.*

## SESSION FOUR: THE BRAND VOICE GUIDE

The scenario: you need a brand voice guide. A document that captures how the brand sounds in writing so clearly that anyone, including Claude in future sessions, can produce on-brand copy without needing to ask you what on-brand means.

This session is different from the others because Claude is helping you develop the thinking *behind* the output. The brand voice guide is as much a discovery process as a writing process.

### Starting with What You Know

OPENING:

```
I want to build a brand voice guide
for [BRAND]. I have some instincts
about the voice but I haven't
```

```
formalized them. I want to use this session to develop the thinking and then document it.

Here's what I know about how the brand sounds: [3-5 sentences of instinct, rough description, adjectives, anything you have].

Here's what I know about how it doesn't sound: [things you've seen in the category that feel wrong for this brand].

Ask me questions if you need more to work with. I'd rather develop this through conversation than try to dump everything upfront.
```

That last sentence is important. It invites Claude to participate as opposed to putting all the burden of context-loading solely on you before the session begins. For a task like brand voice development, where part of what you're doing is strategically thinking through a problem, that collaborative mode produces better results than a fully pre-loaded brief.

## How the Session Develops

Claude will typically respond with a few clarifying questions: who are the customers, what are the reference points, what does the brand stand for beyond the product category. These questions are productive because answering them forces you to articulate things you may have felt but never said.

After a few exchanges, Claude produces a first draft of the voice guide. It has sections for tone adjectives, do's and don'ts, example phrases, and often a brief character description of the brand as if it were a person. That last section is almost always the most useful because it gives you a concrete, imaginable reference point for every future piece of writing.

The refinement pass here is usually about precision. The adjectives Claude chose are close but not exact. You push on each one: not *reserved*, actually more like *measured*. Not *clever*, actually more like *dry*. The distinction matters because the voice guide will be used to make judgment calls on real copy, and close is not good enough for a judgment-call document.

What you end up with, after 45 minutes to an hour, is a voice guide that you actually believe in. You didn't have to pay someone else to produce a generic "about me" sheet that loosely understands your brand.

Instead, you get a document that captures thinking you developed in the session and that reflects your actual instincts, formalized and made portable.

## WHAT ALL FOUR SESSIONS TEACH

Reading across these four session types, a few patterns are worth naming explicitly.

The first output is never the final product. In every session, the first output is a starting point that reveals what Claude understood and what it still needs. Treating the first output as close enough is the most common way to leave real quality on the table.

Pushback is part of the process. The sessions that produced the best outputs were the ones where I challenged a choice, asked for a different angle, or pointed out specifically what wasn't working. Claude engages with real pushback, and that begets results.

Emotional and relational context is as important as business context. The vendor negotiation email session is the clearest example of this, but it's true across all four. When the stakes involve a relationship, a reputation, or a specific human dynamic, that context belongs in the setup.

Sessions then end with a finished output that came from a real conversation. That's the promise of the operator approach, and these four session types are where you can see it being kept.

# CHAPTER SIX

## Iterating Like a Pro

*Why your first response is never the final product, and how to close the gap without starting over*

There is a special circle of AI hell reserved for the moment when Claude hands you something almost right. Not wrong enough to be useless. Not right enough to be done. Just close. And prompting isn't a game of horseshoes.

Most people respond to close by starting over. They write a new prompt, try a different angle, hope this version gets them further. Sometimes it does. More often they end up with a different version of almost right, and the cycle repeats.

Real iteration is forward motion—cold-eyed, surgical, and relentless. It treats the first output as reconnaissance. This chapter arms you with the tactics that turn reconnaissance into victory without resetting the entire battlefield. How to close the gap between the first output and the finished one in as few exchanges as possible, with as little wasted motion as possible. And how to recognize when a different approach, rather than more refinement, is actually what the situation calls for.

## THE REFINEMENT MINDSET

Before we get into specific techniques, there's a mindset shift worth naming. When you receive a first output from Claude, your job is to read it as a diagnosis as opposed to a finished product.

Every first output tells you something. It tells you what Claude understood about your request. It tells you which parts of your context it weighted most heavily. It tells you where it made assumptions, because those are the places where the output diverges from what you actually needed. Reading for these signals, rather than reading for final quality, changes how you respond.

A useful first read-through asks three questions. What's working that should be preserved? What's not working, and can I name specifically why? And what's missing that I didn't include in my setup but clearly needed to?

Those three questions produce a refinement prompt that is targeted and efficient. Simply saying "make it better" gives Claude nothing to work with. Instead, say here is what to keep, here is what to change and why, here is what I forgot to tell you. That kind of prompt produces a second version that is genuinely better, not just different.

## FIVE REFINEMENT TECHNIQUES

The following five specific techniques are for refining Claude's output. They are not mutually exclusive. A single refinement prompt often combines two or three of them. But naming them separately makes it easier to recognize which one a given situation calls for.

### 1. The Surgical Fix

Use this when most of the output is right and one specific part isn't. The surgical fix targets exactly what needs to change without touching anything else.

EXAMPLE:

```
Everything works except the opening
paragraph. It's too soft. I need it
to establish authority immediately,
not build to it. Please rewrite only
the opening paragraph. Leave
everything else as is.
```

The phrase "leave everything else as is" is load-bearing. Without it, Claude may take the rewrite as an invitation to revisit the whole piece. With it, the scope is controlled and the refinement genuinely removes only the parts you want excised.

Surgical fixes are underused because people assume that pointing out one problem implies permission to fix everything. It doesn't. Claude responds precisely to precise instructions. If you want one paragraph rewritten, say so. You'll get one paragraph rewritten.

### 2. The Reframe

Use this when the output is technically correct but approaches the problem from the wrong angle. The reframe is about redirecting the entire approach so you get the result you desire.

EXAMPLE:

```
This is well-written but it's approaching the pitch from a product angle. I need it to come from a customer angle. Instead of leading with what the product is, lead with the problem the customer has before they find it. Same facts, different frame. Please rewrite with that shift.
```

Reframes are most useful when you can't articulate exactly what's wrong with the output but you know it's not landing the way you need it to. Often what feels off is not the execution but the premise. The reframe lets you correct the premise without discarding the work.

### 3. The Constraint Addition

Use this when the output is good but verbose in the way AI is known to be verbose. You forgot to specify a length limit and now the output is twice as long as it needs to be. You didn't mention a channel requirement and the copy reads well on a page but wouldn't work as a caption. The constraint addition adds the boundary you forgot.

EXAMPLE:

```
This is strong. Now cut it to 120 words without losing the core argument. Prioritize the specific detail in the second paragraph over the general framing in the first.
```

Note that the constraint addition here also tells Claude what to prioritize when making cuts. That's important. Without it, Claude will make cuts based on its own judgment about what matters most. Sometimes that judgment is right, but for those times when you have a strong preference about what survives the cut, say so.

**4. The Role Switch**

Use this when you need a different kind of intelligence applied to the same material. The role switch asks Claude to put on a different hat and evaluate or rewrite from that perspective.

EXAMPLES:

```
Now read this as the investor receiving it, not as the person who wrote it. What would make you hesitate to respond? What's the weakest claim in here?
```

```
Switch roles. You're now a skeptical editor who thinks this piece is 30% too long and the real argument doesn't start until the third paragraph. Tell me what you'd cut and why.
```

```
Read this as a first-time customer who has never heard of the brand.
```

```
What questions does this copy leave
unanswered that would prevent them
from buying?
```

The role switch is particularly powerful because it forces a perspective shift that you, as the person too close to the work, may not be able to make yourself. You know what you meant. Claude, reading it from a fresh angle, can tell you whether what you meant is what you said.

**5. The Self-Critique**

Use this when you want Claude to evaluate its own output before you do. The self-critique asks Claude to apply its own judgment to what it just produced, which often surfaces problems more quickly than you'd find them yourself.

EXAMPLES:

```
Before I read this carefully, tell
me: what's the weakest part of what
you just wrote, and why?
```

```
If you were the editor on this
piece, what would you flag for
revision?
```

```
What assumption did you make in
writing this that I might disagree
with?
```

The self-critique works because Claude genuinely engages with it. Instead of saying "everything looks good," it identifies real weaknesses, flags assumptions, and often surfaces considerations that neither of you had foregrounded in the original exchange. This second opinion is usually one worth having.

## HOW TO GIVE FEEDBACK THAT ACTUALLY WORKS

The quality of your refinement prompts determines the quality of your refinement. Vague feedback produces vague revisions. Specific feedback produces specific improvements. This seems obvious but it's consistently where the process breaks down.

Vague feedback sounds like: *this isn't quite right. Make it better. This feels off. Can you punch it up a bit?* These instructions give Claude permission to change things but no information about what to change or in what direction. What you get back will be different, but may not be better.

Specific feedback sounds like:

*The third sentence in the second paragraph is doing two things at once and it's not doing either of them well. Split it.*

*The transition between the second and third sections feels abrupt. I need a bridge sentence.*

*The closing is too soft for the tone established in the opening. The last line should land harder.*

The difference is that specific feedback contains the diagnosis. It tells Claude not just that something is wrong but what is wrong, where it is, and in what direction to fix it. Claude can act on that immediately and precisely.

> *Think of your refinement prompt as a brief to an editor, not a complaint to a service provider. The editor needs to know what you're trying to accomplish, what's in the way, and what good looks like. The service provider just needs to know you're not satisfied.*

One technique that consistently produces better refinement prompts: before you write the feedback, say out loud, or type in a scratch document, what specifically isn't working and why. The act of articulating it, even roughly, forces the specificity that makes the feedback useful. Then distill that articulation into your prompt.

## WHEN TO ITERATE AND WHEN TO START OVER

Sometimes the first output is far enough from what you need that refinement is not the efficient path. Knowing when to cut your losses and reset is as important as knowing how to refine.

The signal that you should start over is usually one of two things. Either the output is structurally wrong, meaning it's the right words organized in the wrong way around the wrong premise, and no amount of targeted fixing will address that. Or the context you loaded at the start was missing something so fundamental that everything built on top of it is skewed.

When the structure is wrong, reframing sometimes helps. But if you've tried a reframe and the output is still organized around the wrong premise, starting over with a more explicit structural instruction is faster than continuing to push against a foundation that isn't going to move.

When the context was missing something fundamental, the fix is to add the missing context explicitly and ask Claude to regenerate from scratch with that addition. You might say: *I realize I didn't tell you something important at the start. [Missing information]. With that in mind, please start the whole piece over rather than patching the current version.*

Starting over is sometimes necessary. View it as recalibration instead of failure. Even Stephen Curry hits the back rim a few times in a row and needs a tweak to his shooting motion to hit nothing but net again.

The best operators know the difference between a session that needs one more targeted pass and a session that needs to be reset. That judgment comes with practice, and it saves an enormous amount of time once you have it.

## THE DIMINISHING RETURNS PROBLEM

There is a point in every iterative session beyond which continued refinement produces less improvement per exchange, just as there is a point when it's time to put that pint of chocolate ice cream back in the freezer.

The first refinement pass typically produces a large jump in quality. The second produces a meaningful improvement. By the fourth or fifth, you are usually moving single words and adjusting commas, and the question you should be asking is whether I should be setting an earlier alarm to hit the gym or start exercising more dietary self-control.

Claude is not always the right tool for the final 10%. Sometimes the final 10% is a judgment call about voice, rhythm, or precision that you are better positioned to make yourself with 30 seconds of direct editing than you are to communicate to Claude in two minutes of instruction.

Knowing when to take the wheel is part of the skill. The operator approach does not mean delegating everything to Claude. It means using Claude for the parts of the work where it creates leverage, and doing the parts yourself where your own judgment is faster and more precise than the instruction overhead required to get Claude there.

The goal of an iterative session is to create a finished, high-quality piece of work. Sometimes those are the same thing. Often the most efficient path to the latter involves Claude getting you 90% of the way there and then slamming home the alley-oop yourself.

## BUILDING AN ITERATION HABIT

The techniques in this chapter become fast with practice. The first few times you use the self-critique or the role switch, they will feel deliberate. After a dozen sessions, they become instinctive. You will read a first output and immediately know which technique the situation calls for.

The habit worth building is this: before you send any refinement prompt, spend 15 seconds naming what specifically isn't working, where it is, and what direction the fix should go. That 15 seconds of diagnosis produces refinement prompts that are two or three times more effective than prompts written without it.

A small amount of diagnosis. A targeted prompt. A better output. Repeat until done. Carve your Hall-of-Fame bust.

That's what iterating like a pro actually looks like: a disciplined practice of reading carefully, diagnosing specifically, and communicating precisely. Applied consistently, it will close the gap between what Claude first produces and what you actually need faster than any other approach in this book.

# CHAPTER SEVEN

## Prompting for Voice

*The hardest thing to get right with AI, and how to stop settling for a reasonable facsimile of yourself*

Voice is the thing that makes writing yours. Claude will provide you an ocean of information, structure, and ideas. But the way your sentences slither, the rhythm you use to build to a point, or the words you reach for in your vocabulary toolkit are all uniquely and unabashedly yours. All of it together produces something that, when it's working, is unmistakably you.

It is also the single hardest thing to get right with AI. Voice is harder to pin down because most people have never been forced to articulate what their voice actually is. You know it when you hear it. When words on a page read like the best version of yourself is literally speaking to you, pop a bottle of your favorite champagne. Because that elusive voice has been officially found.

Working with Claude on voice-sensitive writing forces you to do something most writers never do: externalize what makes your writing yours and translate it into instructions a highly capable collaborator can execute. That is a specific skill, and most people skip it entirely, which is why most AI-assisted writing sounds like it was produced by a very well-read committee who overly relies on the em-dash.

This chapter teaches you how to train Claude on yours within a session, how to use the persona lock technique to hold that voice across extended work, and how to apply it across three distinct contexts: your personal voice, your brand's voice, and a character's voice in creative work.

## WHAT VOICE ACTUALLY IS

Before you can teach Claude your voice, you need to understand what you're actually teaching. Most people describe voice in adjectives like *confident, dry, direct, warm, irreverent*. Those adjectives are a starting point. You need more. Embrace your inner Edgar asking for a glass of sugar in water. "More."

Voice lives in five specific dimensions, and understanding them gives you the raw material for voice instructions that Claude can actually act on rather than approximate.

**Sentence length and variation.**

Do you build long, subordinated sentences that gather force as they move, or do you prefer short declarative ones that land and get out? Do you vary length deliberately for rhythm, or do you default to a consistent register? This is one of the most immediately identifiable elements of any writer's voice.

**Relationship to the reader.**

How close do you stand? Do you address the reader directly and often, or do you write as though you're thinking out loud and the reader is listening in? Do you assume they already know things, or do you explain carefully? The assumed intimacy between writer and reader is a major architectural element of voice that almost nobody names when describing theirs.

**Attitude toward the subject.**

Are you certain or exploratory? Do you stake positions or present options? Do you lean into complexity or cut through it as fast as possible? Writers who value directness and writers who value nuance both describe their voices similarly, but the writing sounds completely different.

**Vocabulary selection**.

Do you reach for the Latin word or the Greek one? Do you default to the concrete and physical or the abstract and structural? The vocabulary you instinctively deploy is one of the sharpest signals of voice and one Claude can calibrate precisely once you give it examples.

**What you refuse to do**.

This is the dimension almost no one mentions and it is often the most defining. Every distinctive writer has things they won't do like won't use certain transitions, won't moralize at the close, won't explain the joke, won't soften a landing that should hit hard. The negative space of a voice is as defining as what fills it.

> *Describing your voice in adjectives tells Claude the destination. Showing Claude actual samples of your writing tells it the route. You need both. Neither one alone gets you there.*

## TEACHING CLAUDE YOUR VOICE

The most reliable method is the simplest: show Claude your writing. Give it three to five representative samples, each a few paragraphs long, covering different content types if you have them. The variety helps Claude identify what is consistent across contexts rather than what is simply a product of one particular piece.

The prompt structure that works:

VOICE TRAINING PROMPT:

```
I'm going to show you several samples of my writing. Your job is to study them carefully and identify what makes the voice consistent across all of them. After you've read them, I'm going to ask you to write in this voice. Don't summarize the content. Focus entirely on the style: sentence structure, rhythm, vocabulary choices, relationship to the reader, what I do and don't do.

Sample 1: [PASTE WRITING SAMPLE]

Sample 2: [PASTE WRITING SAMPLE]
```

```
Sample 3: [PASTE WRITING SAMPLE]

After reading these, describe back
to me what you observe about the
voice. Then I'll give you the task.
```

That last instruction—asking Claude to describe the voice before writing in it—is the step most people skip and the one that matters most. When Claude articulates what it observed, you find out whether it read you correctly before it writes three pages in the wrong register. If it missed something important, you correct it before the draft begins. If it nailed it, pour yourself another glass of that champagne.

After Claude describes the voice and you confirm or correct the read, the task prompt is clean:

TASK PROMPT AFTER VOICE TRAINING:

```
Good. Hold that voice. Now write
[SPECIFIC TASK] in exactly that
voice. Do not default to a generic
writing style. Stay in the voice we
just established.
```

That last line is critical. Without it, Claude sometimes drifts back toward its trained defaults on task types it has seen a thousand times. The instruction keeps the voice foregrounded rather than letting familiarity override it.

## THE PERSONA LOCK

A single voice-training exchange at the start of a session is usually enough to hold the voice for that session. Claude maintains context, and the samples you loaded stay in play.

The problem is that sessions end. The next day you open a fresh conversation and Claude remembers nothing. You'd have to re-train the voice from scratch every time, which is tedious enough that most people stop doing it.

The persona lock solves this. It is a compact, portable voice document you paste into the top of any new session to immediately establish the voice without running a full training exercise. One investment yields infinite deployments.

A persona lock runs one to two pages and contains three things: a concise description of the voice in the writer's own terms, a set of specific do's and don'ts derived from studying the actual writing, and two or three short example passages that demonstrate the voice in action.

Deploying it looks like this:

```
PERSONA LOCK DEPLOYMENT:

Before we begin, here is the voice
guide for [NAME/BRAND]. Please read
it carefully and hold this voice for
everything you write in this
session.

[PASTE PERSONA LOCK DOCUMENT]

Confirm you've read it and tell me
the two or three things that feel
most distinctive about this voice.
Then we'll get to work.
```

The confirmation step is essential. It is a rapid diagnostic that catches misreadings before they compound into a full draft. Claude will occasionally anchor on the wrong element of the persona lock, and catching that in two sentences is considerably less painful than catching it after 800 words. Do not skip this step.

Building a persona lock for your own voice is worth a focused hour. You do it once, refine it as your voice evolves, and every session that requires you to sound like yourself becomes immediately more productive. This is one of the highest-return investments in your entire Claude workflow.

## YOUR PERSONAL VOICE: THE HARDEST CASE

Personal voice is the most individual and the hardest to teach because you never designed it. It evolved over years of thinking, speaking, and writing without conscious engineering, which means you have less conscious access to what it actually consists of than you probably think. Try explaining to someone who's never driven a car how your hands move the steering wheel when making a left turn, and you'll understand my point.

The samples-first method above works best for personal voice, with one small addition: before you paste in the samples, write a one-paragraph description of how you think you write. Then compare that description to what Claude observes.

This comparison almost always indicates the gap between how you think you write and how you actually write, and that gap contains information. The places where your self-description diverges from Claude's observation are where your voice has characteristics you haven't fully recognized in yourself. Those characteristics are often the most distinctive parts of your voice, and knowing what they are lets you protect and deploy them deliberately instead of hoping they survive the process.

A writer who describes their voice as direct and no-nonsense might discover through this exercise that they open almost everything with a scene or a provocation before making the point, and that this approach is one of the most recognizable things about how they write. If that's the case for you, then that style is worth preserving.

## BRAND VOICE: WRITING AS THE BRAND

Brand voice is a different problem. Where personal voice is discovered and described, brand voice is often constructed and must then be made portable enough for anyone, including Claude across many sessions, to execute consistently.

A brand voice guide goes deeper than a brand brief. The brief covers what the brand is. The voice guide covers how it writes, including the edge cases that test the voice and expose generic guidelines for the wishful thinking they usually are.

The most useful additions in a voice guide are worked examples for specific difficult situations. Train Claude on how your brand handles a product problem, a public complaint, a price increase, a competitor gaining ground. These are the moments where generic voice guidelines collapse and where specific, worked examples become the only thing that actually helps.

EDGE CASE EXAMPLE FOR A BRAND VOICE GUIDE:

```
When addressing a product issue or
delay:

Right: 'We found a problem with the
current batch and pulled it. A new
run ships in three weeks. If you're
waiting on an order, we'll reach out
directly.'

Wrong: 'We sincerely apologize for
any inconvenience this may have
caused. We are working diligently to
resolve this issue and appreciate
your patience and understanding.'
```

```
The difference: the brand owns
problems directly, uses plain
language, gives specifics, and does
not perform contrition. It treats
the customer as an adult who wants
information, not reassurance.
```

One worked example like that is worth a dozen bullet points of adjective-based voice description. It shows rather than tells, and Claude can extrapolate from it to situations you haven't explicitly anticipated. The goal is not to pre-answer every possible scenario, but to make the brand's logic clear enough that Claude can reason its way to the right answer on its own.

### CHARACTER VOICE IN CREATIVE WORK

Character voice is where the stakes are highest and the craft is most demanding. A character's voice is not just how they talk. It's how they see, view, hear, and live. What do they notice, what slides past them, what do they find funny, what makes them go cold? Voice in fiction is inseparable from character, and teaching Claude a character voice means teaching it a character.

The most effective character voice prompt combines three elements: a character description that goes well beyond appearance and backstory into psychological disposition and worldview, a set of speech and thought patterns with specific examples, and a reference passage written in the character's voice that Claude can use as a calibration point.

```
CHARACTER VOICE SETUP:

The character is [NAME]. Here is what you need to write in their voice.

Who they are: [Background, age, context, role in the story]

How they see the world: [Worldview, what they value, what they distrust, how they interpret events]

How they speak and think: [Sentence patterns, vocabulary level, use of humor or irony, emotional register, what they say directly vs. what they leave unsaid]

What they would never say or do: [The edges of the character that define them by contrast]
```

```
Reference passage in their voice: [A
paragraph or two you've written for
this character, or that captures the
register exactly]
```

The reference passage is the load-bearing element. A character described as sardonic and world-weary can be written a hundred different ways. A character whose reference passage shows how that sardonic worldview expresses itself in the way they describe getting stuck in traffic leaves almost no room for interpretation. Claude has a specific texture to anchor to.

For extended creative projects, the character voice document becomes one of your most valuable working assets. Each new session, you paste it in and pick up where you left off. The character stays coherent across time and across the inherent amnesia of session-based AI work.

## WHEN VOICE DRIFTS AND HOW TO CATCH IT

Even with a solid voice setup, drift happens. It shows up most in long sessions, when the voice established early starts competing with a lot of subsequent material for Claude's active attention. The defaults begin to reassert themselves. The sentences get slightly more generic. The characteristic analogies appear less frequently. If you're reading carefully, you catch it early. If you're moving fast, you don't notice until half a page has gone sideways.

The fix is fast:

REANCHORING PROMPT:

```
I'm noticing the voice drifting. Let's reanchor. This is [NAME]'s voice: [Two or three sentences capturing the most distinctive elements]. Stay in that voice from here.
```

Learning to notice drift early and reanchor quickly is one of the marks of a skilled Claude operator, because it costs all of 10 seconds and it saves you from the alternative, which is discovering the drift after significant output has accumulated in the wrong register and having to painstakingly go back through it.

## THE HONEST LIMIT

Let me tell you what Claude actually can and cannot do here, because this chapter should not leave you with unrealistic expectations.

Claude can learn a voice well enough to produce writing that is consistent with it, on-brand, recognizably in the established style. It can do this reliably at a quality that is genuinely useful for most professional purposes.

What it cannot do is produce writing that is indistinguishable from your best work. Your best work has something in it that comes from you being you: the observations that only you would make, the connection that only exists because of your specific life experiences, the line that lands because the writer genuinely thinks it and believes it.

Claude has only a model of your voice. The model is good. It is not your brain matter itself.

The most effective use of Claude for voice-sensitive writing is as a capable first-draft producer working in your established style. The drafts are worth your editing time. Your editing is where your actual voice, the parts Claude cannot reach, gets added back in. You are using the machine to give yourself something worth working on and then doing the work to create a final product worth reading.

AI-generated copy is the floor, not the ceiling. Your voice, applied on top of what Claude produces, is what makes it yours.

# CHAPTER EIGHT

## Claude for Brand Building

*How to use AI to develop the stories, positioning, and copy that turn products into brands*

There is a difference between a product and a brand, and most people who make things feel it before they can explain it. A product is what you sell. A brand is why someone drives past three other options to get to yours, buys it again without being reminded, and tells people about it at dinner as if it's something they created themselves. That gap gets closed by story, positioning, voice, and consistent communication stacked over time.

This is where Claude earns its keep for founders, because it helps you surface, articulate, and communicate the meaning that is already sitting inside what you're building. If you have a real story, real beliefs, and a real reason to exist in a crowded category, Claude can help you find the language for all of it. If you don't have those things, no amount of AI-assisted copy will paper over the absence.

This chapter assumes you have a product or service worth building a brand around. Here's how to use Claude to do the building.

## THE ORIGIN STORY

Every brand has an origin story. Almost every founder tells theirs badly.

They either drown you in operational detail that nobody outside the building cares about, or they reach for the language they've seen other brands use and produce something that sounds like a press release written by a committee that's never tasted the product.

The origin story is the most important piece of brand writing you will ever produce. Think of it as a superhero movie. If the origin story stinks, the film probably will too. It is the foundation everything else gets stacked on top of. It answers the question every new customer is actually asking: why does this exist, and why should I trust the person who made it?

Claude is particularly useful here because it can help you pull the story out of your experience rather than fabricate something on top of it. The session structure that works best is conversational: you talk, Claude asks questions, and between the two of you the real story gets excavated.

ORIGIN STORY SESSION OPENER:

```
I need to develop the origin story
for [BRAND]. I'm going to tell you
how this brand came to exist, and I
want you to ask me questions that
help surface the details that make
it worth telling. Don't write
anything yet. Just ask.

Here's the rough version: [Tell it
in your own words, as plainly as
possible, without trying to make it
sound like a brand story yet]
```

What Claude asks next will likely surprise you. It will find the moment you glossed over because it seemed ordinary. The detail you left out because you assumed everyone already knew it. The belief embedded in a decision you made three years ago that you've never actually named out loud.

A few exchanges of questions and answers and you'll have more usable raw material than most founders accumulate in years of telling their story at trade shows and investor meetings. Then you ask Claude to draft it, specifying the format: 200 words for the About page, 500 for the pitch deck, 50 for the back panel of the bottle. Each is a different craft problem. Having developed the full story first makes all three faster, better, and more cohesive.

## POSITIONING: FINDING WHAT'S ACTUALLY YOURS

Positioning is the answer to one question: *in the mind of the customer you most want, what is the single thing that makes you the right choice over every alternative?*

Most founders get this wrong in one of three predictable ways. Either they list multiple things instead of committing to one, they describe a feature when positioning requires a benefit, or they say something true but generic, something every premium brand in every category claims, like better ingredients or more care in the process.

Claude is useful for positioning work specifically because it can challenge your answer the way a skeptical buyer actually would. The most productive positioning session is structured as an interrogation, not a collaboration.

### POSITIONING PRESSURE-TEST SESSION:

```
I'm going to tell you how I think [BRAND] is positioned, and I want you to challenge it as aggressively as you honestly can. Play the role of a category buyer who has heard a hundred pitches and is deeply skeptical of claims that sound like everyone else's.

My positioning: [STATE IT AS PLAINLY AS POSSIBLE]

Push back hard. If my differentiator is actually generic, tell me. If I'm describing a feature when I should be describing a benefit, call it out. If there's a sharper version of what I'm trying to say, surface it.
```

What comes back from a session like this can be uncomfortable and valuable in roughly equal measure. Claude will find the places where your positioning is soft. It will identify the claims that sound specific but aren't. It will push you toward the version of your differentiator that is actually defensible, ownable, and meaningful to a real person with real options.

The loop usually takes somewhere between three and five exchanges. You start with a claim, Claude challenges it. You sharpen it. Claude challenges the sharper version so you refine again. By the fourth exchange you usually have something you can actually build on.

> *Positioning is not what you want to be known for. It is what you can credibly claim and no one else can easily take from you. Claude helps you find the difference between those two things.*

## TAGLINES AND BRAND LANGUAGE

A tagline is the compression of the entire brand's positioning into the fewest possible words. It is the hardest piece of copy to write and the one that has to survive the longest.

Claude generates tagline options fast, which is both the value and the trap. The value is volume, which increases the odds of something genuinely good surfacing. Next, you'll have to do the judging.

The session structure that produces the best tagline work is iterative and specific about what's wrong with each round.

TAGLINE DEVELOPMENT SESSION:

```
Generate 15 tagline options for [BRAND].

Brand brief: [PASTE]

Positioning: [STATE IT]

Constraints: No more than six words. No question marks. No exclamation points. Do not use any of these words: [LIST]. Do not sacrifice clarity for cleverness.
```

Read the 15 taglines. Some will be immediately wrong. Some will be close. Occasionally one will stop you cold. Take the two or three nearest the target and tell Claude specifically what is working and what is missing in each.

REFINEMENT PROMPT:

```
Option 3 is closest. The structure is right but the last word is too
```

```
generic. Option 9 has the right
energy but it's a word too long and
the second word is doing nothing.
Option 12 is interesting but it
could belong to any brand in the
category.

Generate 10 more that build on
what's working in 3 and 9 while
fixing what's wrong. Stay in the
same territory.
```

Repeat until something lands. Brand language gets made in the iteration, not the first generation.

## PRODUCT POSITIONING AND LAUNCH COPY

Brand positioning is the umbrella. Product positioning is what you're keeping dry when it rains: what this specific item is, who it's for, why it exists in the line, and what it does that the other products don't.

Product copy, the descriptions on your website, your packaging, your retail sell sheets, is where brand positioning touches real customers at the item level. It is where the abstract claims of the brand get made concrete and specific.

For physical products, load sensory detail before you ask for a single word of copy. This is the step almost everyone skips, and it's why so much product copy sounds like it was written by someone who has never opened the package.

```
SENSORY CONTEXT FOR PRODUCT COPY:

Before writing any copy, here is the sensory profile of [PRODUCT]:

Appearance: [Color, texture, viscosity, visual character]

Aroma: [What you smell first, what develops, what it evokes]

Flavor/Feel: [Initial impression, development, finish, heat timeline if applicable]

Use context: [What people reach for it with, when, what experience it creates]
```

That sensory grounding is the difference between copy that describes a product and copy that makes someone want to open it. "A bold, complex sauce with lingering heat" is a description. Copy built from actual sensory detail makes the reader feel what it's like to use it before they've bought it, and that type of copy converts readers into satisfied buyers.

## THE MYTHOLOGY LAYER

The brands that build real followings that develop something approaching a cult in their categories, have a layer beneath the product and the copy that most brands never bother to build. It is a belief system about why the category matters, what is wrong with how most of it gets done, and what a better version looks like.

It is a worldview disguised as a marketing strategy. The brand exists to express it.

This is one of the most underestimated applications of Claude for brand builders, and one of the most powerful, because good mythology is a reflection of good thinking, and Claude's ability to help you develop and articulate thinking is where it creates its most distinctive leverage.

MYTHOLOGY DEVELOPMENT SESSION:

```
I want to develop the mythology for
[BRAND]. Not the marketing story.
The actual belief system.
```

```
Here are some things I believe about
[CATEGORY] that most people in the
category would never say out loud:
[LIST 3-5 GENUINE BELIEFS, AS
HONESTLY AS YOU CAN STATE THEM]

Here is what I think is wrong with
how most brands in this category
operate: [BE SPECIFIC]

Here is what I think the category
could be at its best, and almost
never is: [YOUR GENUINE VISION]

Work with what I've given you. Ask
me questions to deepen it. Then help
me develop this into a mythology
document: a statement of beliefs
about the category that could serve
as the philosophical foundation of
the brand.
```

What comes out of this session is the document that makes all future copy easier to write, because every piece is now an expression of a coherent point of view rather than a standalone attempt to sound interesting.

It also gives you something to test new work against. Does this copy express what we actually believe? Does this campaign feel consistent with the worldview this brand represents? Those questions become answerable. Without the mythology document, they're just vibes.

## AI-GENERATED VS. AI-ASSISTED COPY

The distinction in this chapter's title is worth sitting with before you close it.

AI-generated copy is copy Claude wrote and you published. It may or may not be competent, but it is certainly not yours. It does not carry your perspective, your specificity, your actual conviction about the category. Readers may not notice it in a one-off reading, but across hundreds of pieces over time, they will feel the absence of a real person behind it even if they can't name what's missing.

AI-assisted copy is copy that emerged from a real session where you brought the knowledge and perspective, and Claude helped you find the language for it. The fingerprints of your thinking are all over the structure AI built. That creates substance that customers will resonate with.

Every session in this chapter is designed to produce what resonates. The mythology session requires you to state what you actually believe. The origin story session requires you to tell what actually happened. The positioning session requires you to defend a claim you genuinely think is true. Claude cannot generate any of that. You have to bring it.

What Claude gives you in return is the ability to develop that material faster, test it harder, and express it more precisely than you could working alone.

Have something worth saying, and Claude will help you say it in a way that makes people listen.

# CHAPTER NINE

## Claude for Operations

*Turning the unglamorous work into a system that actually runs*

There's a reason nobody writes books about operations. The machinery that keeps a business running is not the subject of inspiration. Most founders tolerate it. Some resent it. Almost nobody talks about it at conferences. This is why there are no bestsellers about production planning or vendor communication or process documentation.

Operations work is detail-heavy, repetitive, and punishing when you're not paying attention. A missed production timeline compounds. A vendor communication handled badly festers like an open wound acquired traversing Fury Road. A process that lives only in your head becomes a chokepoint the moment your business grows past what your head can hold.

Claude, for all intents and purposes, is your digital Furiosa. What it does is make operations faster, more precise, and less dependent on your bandwidth. It turns the work you tolerate into work you move through. For a solo operator running multiple entities, that is the difference between keeping up and getting tied to a tree to become vulture fodder.

This chapter covers the operational applications where Claude creates the most leverage: production planning, vendor communication, cost estimation, proposal writing, and process documentation. Each one has a specific session structure and specific leverage points worth knowing.

## PRODUCTION PLANNING

Production planning is a coordination problem. You have a product to make, inputs that need to arrive at the right time, a manufacturer with their own lead times, a target inventory level, and a date you're working backward from. The variables interact in ways that are easy to track when there's one of them and easy to lose when there are six.

The most useful thing Claude does in production planning is to create structure. It takes a pile of variables and constraints and builds a coherent timeline with dependencies mapped and risk points flagged. It catches the conflict between your label printer's lead time and your manufacturer's deposit deadline before that conflict becomes a crisis.

PRODUCTION PLANNING SESSION OPENER:

```
I need to plan a production run for [PRODUCT]. Here are the variables:

Target quantity: [X units]

Target in-hand date: [DATE]

Manufacturer lead time: [X weeks from approved artwork and deposit]

Label printer lead time: [X weeks from approved artwork]

Artwork revision rounds: typically [X weeks]

Deposit required: [X%] upfront, balance on delivery

Current inventory: [X units], selling at approximately [X units/month]

Build a backward timeline from the in-hand date with all dependencies mapped. Flag any points where the
```

```
timeline is tight and tell me what
the risk is at each of those points.
```

What comes back is a structured timeline with explicit dependencies and flagged risk points. It gives you a clear, readable plan that captures everything you loaded and organizes it so you can act on it today. You don't even have to worry if it will have car troubles on its way to work.

The follow-up passes are where the real planning happens: what if the label printer takes an extra week, what's the minimum viable inventory level before the run needs to start, how does the timeline shift if you cut the quantity by 20%. Claude holds the full context of the plan across *all of it.*

## VENDOR COMMUNICATION

Vendor communication is one of those categories of business writing where the stakes are higher than they look. The email you send to a manufacturer or supplier is a representation of how you operate. Vendors work with a lot of companies. They remember the ones who communicate clearly and follow through. They also remember the ones who don't.

Claude is useful here for both the drafting and the thinking before the drafting. The most valuable prompt you can write before a difficult vendor email is the brief that forces you to figure out what you actually want the communication to accomplish.

### The Pre-Draft Brief

```
PRE-DRAFT BRIEF:

I need to write an email to [VENDOR/CONTACT]. Before we draft anything, help me think through the communication.


Situation: [What's happened or what you need]

Relationship: [How long, what the dynamic is, any relevant history]

What I want from this communication: [Be specific about the outcome, not just the message]

What I want to avoid: [Relationship damage, bad precedent, looking weak or desperate]

Leverage I have: [Be honest]

Leverage they have: [Be honest too]
```

```
Before drafting: is there anything in this situation I might be missing? Any risk in the approach I'm describing?
```

That last question is where the real value lives. Claude will occasionally surface something you had not considered: a way the email could be misread, a precedent it might set, a reframe of the vendor's likely perspective that changes how the communication should be approached. While this feature might not seem always useful, it can occasionally flag a potential relationship-ruining mistake.

### The Follow-Up and Escalation

Two vendor communication scenarios come up often enough to deserve their own structures.

The follow-up, when someone has not responded, needs to re-establish the thread without making the other person defensive. Short, easy to respond to, no passive aggression leaking through the professionalism.

FOLLOW-UP PROMPT:

```
I sent [VENDOR] an email [X days] ago about [TOPIC]. No response.
```

```
Draft a follow-up that re-establishes the thread without sounding impatient or passive-aggressive. Keep it short. Make it easy for them to respond.

Context: [Original ask, timeline pressure, relationship dynamic]
```

The escalation, when something has gone wrong and needs to be addressed directly, requires a different balance. Clear about the problem. Specific about what you need. Firm about the stakes, but not so hot that it makes a recoverable situation unrecoverable. This is the communication that is hardest to write when you are frustrated, which is exactly when you need to write it. Claude's distance from the emotion is an asset here.

## COST ESTIMATION AND FINANCIAL MODELING

Use Claude when you need fast, rough cost estimation that tells you whether an opportunity is worth pursuing before you build a spreadsheet.

The use case: you have a decision in front of you that requires cost context you don't have at your fingertips. For example, a product extension, a new channel, or a new capital expenditure. You need a number accurate enough to tell you whether to keep going.

FAST COST ESTIMATION SESSION:

```
I'm considering [OPPORTUNITY/DECISION]. I need a rough cost model to determine if it's worth pursuing seriously.

What I know: [Variables you have]

What I don't know: [Variables you're uncertain about]

Build a rough model with reasonable assumptions for the unknowns. State every assumption explicitly. Give me a low, mid, and high scenario. Then tell me which variable has the most impact on the outcome and why.
```

State every assumption explicitly is essential language. Without it, Claude builds a model on assumptions you cannot see or evaluate. With it, you know exactly which inputs are real and which are educated guesses, and you know where to focus before making a decision.

The highest-impact variable question is equally important. In most rough models, one or two variables drive most of the outcome. Knowing which ones tells you where to spend your information-gathering time before you commit to anything deeper.

## PROPOSAL WRITING

Proposals come in many forms: wholesale pitches, distributor outreach, co-manufacturing proposals, partnership decks. What they share is that they are persuasion documents, and the most common failure in persuasion documents is leading with what you want instead of what they need.

A wholesale proposal that opens with your brand history is organized around your interests. A wholesale proposal that opens with a gap in their current set and how you fill it is organized around theirs. One of these gets read more carefully. You already know which one.

PROPOSAL STRATEGY SESSION:

```
I'm writing a proposal to [TARGET].
Here's what I know about them:
```

```
[What they sell, who their customers
are, what their current relevant set
looks like, any gaps or
opportunities you've identified]


Here's what I'm proposing: [Your
product, service, or partnership and
the terms]


Before we draft anything: from their
perspective, what is the strongest
case for saying yes? What is the
most likely reason they say no? How
should this proposal be organized to
lead with their interests rather
than mine?
```

The structural recommendation that comes back from this session is almost always different from how the founder would have opened the proposal by default. That shift, from your-perspective-first to their-perspective-first, changes the opening, the order of information, and the emphasis throughout.

> *A proposal organized around what you want to say is a document. A proposal*

> *organized around what they need to hear is a tool. Claude helps you build the tool.*

## PROCESS DOCUMENTATION

Process documentation is the most consistently neglected operational task in small businesses, and the one whose neglect costs the most as things grow. When every process lives in your head, you are the bottleneck for every process. The business cannot outrun your personal supervision bandwidth.

Most founders know they should document their processes. Most founders don't, because the immediate cost of stopping to write down how something works feels higher than the deferred cost of not having written it down. Claude helps to lower the friction enough to change the calculus.

The most efficient approach: describe the process to Claude conversationally, the way you'd explain it to a new employee on their first day, and let Claude produce the structured documentation from your description.

PROCESS DOCUMENTATION SESSION:

```
I'm going to describe a process we use in the business. Turn my
```

```
description into a clear,
step-by-step document that someone
who has never done this before could
follow without asking me questions.

Ask me clarifying questions as I go
if something is unclear. When I'm
done describing, draft the document.
Then I'll review and tell you what's
missing.

The process is: [Describe it
conversationally, in order, with as
much detail as you naturally
include]
```

The instruction to ask clarifying questions as you go is doing real work. It means Claude will flag the ambiguities in your description before they become gaps in the documentation. You will get questions like: what happens if the supplier doesn't have the item in stock, who is responsible for this step when you're unavailable, what is the acceptable quality threshold here. Those questions surface the edge cases that make a process document actually usable rather than just technically complete.

A moderately complex process documented through this method takes 20 to 30 minutes total. Without Claude, the same process probably never gets documented at all, because the time cost always felt too high relative to the immediate return.

That calculus shifts. Document the process. Future you will be grateful.

## THE OPERATIONAL MINDSET FOR CLAUDE

Operational work rewards specificity more than almost any other domain. A production timeline built on vague lead times is not a production timeline. A vendor email with no clear ask is not a vendor email. A cost model built on unstated assumptions is not a cost model.

This is actually good news. The discipline of loading specific context before making a request, which Chapter Two established as the foundation of the operator approach, is not extra work in operational sessions. It *is the work*. You are going to need to think through the lead times, the relationship history, the cost variables anyway. Doing that thinking inside a structured Claude session rather than in your head produces two things: a better output and a record of the thinking that produced it.

One of the underappreciated benefits of working through operational problems with Claude is that the session itself becomes documentation. You can refer back to it, share it, or use it as the opening context for the next related session.

Operations built on documented thinking are more resilient than operations built on memory. For a solo operator, it is the difference between a business that can grow and one that is permanently capped by what one person can personally hold in their head.

# CHAPTER TEN

## Claude for Creative Work

*How to use AI as a creative collaborator without losing what makes the work yours*

Creative work is where most people assume AI is least useful. It is where voice matters most, where originality is the entire point, where the difference between something that lands and something that falls flat is often a quality you can feel but cannot manufacture. If Claude cannot reliably produce your voice, as the last chapter argued it cannot, what exactly is it good for here?

Creative work is also where the people who figure out how to use it well get the biggest advantage. Claude operates as a structural partner, a sounding board, a framework builder, and an expander of what you can attempt alone. The creators who use Claude most effectively in creative work are using it to expand their thought process and extend their reach.

This chapter covers four applications: screenplay and script development, storytelling frameworks for fiction and IP, world-building for extended creative universes, and social content calendars that hold a creative voice at scale. Each one has its own session dynamics. Each one has leverage points worth knowing before you sit down to work.

## SCREENPLAY AND SCRIPT DEVELOPMENT

Screenwriting is one of the most structurally demanding forms of writing that exists. It has rules, expectations, and load-bearing requirements. Acts break at specific moments. Scenes do specific work. Characters reveal themselves through action and dialogue. Every page has a job. Deviation from these requirements is possible but expensive. You need to understand the rules deeply before you can break them productively.

Claude understands screenplay structure. Not at the level of a working professional with a decade of produced credits, but well enough to be a useful collaborator for someone developing scripts outside of a professional writing room. The applications divide into three phases that mirror how good development actually works: concept and premise, structural development, and scene and dialogue work.

## Concept and Premise Development

Most script ideas die in the concept phase because the creator cannot yet say what the story is actually about or why the characters matter at the level that makes it worth developing. Getting to a strong log line—a compressed statement of the central dramatic question, the stakes, and the specific protagonist whose journey the audience is following—forces the clarity that makes everything downstream possible.

CONCEPT DEVELOPMENT SESSION:

```
I have an idea for a script and I want to develop it into a strong premise before I start building structure.

Here's the idea as I currently have it: [Describe it without trying to make it sound polished]

Ask me questions. Push on what the central conflict actually is, who the protagonist really is, and what they want versus what they need. Don't write the log line yet. Help me find the answers that will make the log line true rather than just serviceable.
```

The distinction between a log line that is true and one that is merely serviceable is worth sitting with. A serviceable log line describes the plot. A true log line captures what the story is actually about at the level of theme and human experience. The development session does its real work in finding that level, and Claude's questions are usually what get you there.

Once the concept is clear, the log line session moves fast:

LOG LINE SESSION:

```
Based on what we've developed, write five versions of the log line. Each under 35 words. Each should name the protagonist, the central conflict, and what is at stake. Vary the emphasis across the five: some leading with the protagonist's want, some with the external conflict, some with the thematic stakes. I'll tell you which direction is closest.
```

**Structural Development**

Script structure is the architecture of the story: the act breaks, the turning points, the midpoint, the dark night, the climax. Professional writers have built detailed frameworks for this architecture over decades, and Claude knows them. The risk in structural sessions is over-reliance on formulae, so the clever Claude operator uses structural frameworks as a diagnostic, not a template.

STRUCTURE DEVELOPMENT SESSION:

```
I want to develop the structure for [SCRIPT TITLE]. Here is where I am:

Premise: [Log line or premise statement]

What I know exists in this story: [Scenes, moments, or sequences you already have, even if you don't know where they fall]

What I don't know yet: [The structural gaps]

Build a structural map with me. Don't hand me a rigid three-act outline. Find the structure that is native to this particular story. Use what I've given you. Ask me what you need. Push back if you see a structural problem forming.
```

*Find the structure that is native to this particular story* is the most important instruction in that prompt. Formula produces scripts that feel like every other script built on the same formula. The best structural work uses frameworks as diagnostic tools, not molds.

One useful variation is the beat sheet review, where you bring a completed beat sheet and ask Claude to evaluate specific structural problems before drafting begins:

```
BEAT SHEET REVIEW SESSION:

Here is the beat sheet for [TITLE]:
[PASTE]

Evaluate it for three specific
problems: places where the
protagonist is passive rather than
active, places where the emotional
logic breaks down between scenes,
and places where the stakes are not
clearly escalating. Tell me which
problem is most likely to cause the
script to fail if I don't address it
before drafting.
```

## Scene and Dialogue Work

Scene and dialogue work is where Claude's usefulness becomes most conditional on your own craft investment. Claude can write a scene and can write dialogue. What it cannot reliably do is write a scene that sounds like your specific characters in your specific world with the weight that comes from knowing these people across a hundred pages.

The most productive use of Claude at the scene level is developing plotline through questions first, then refining with targeted feedback.

```
SCENE DEVELOPMENT SESSION:

I need to develop a scene. Function in the script: [What this scene needs to accomplish structurally and emotionally]


What I know: [Characters present, location, what happens at the plot level]

What I don't know: [The element giving you trouble]


Before writing anything, ask me questions about what each character wants in this specific moment and what they are hiding. I want to
```

```
understand the subtext before we
write the text.
```

Subtext before text. That one instruction is the difference between dialogue that sounds like real people under pressure and dialogue that sounds like characters saying what the plot requires them to say.

## STORYTELLING FRAMEWORKS

Claude can write fiction, but as an author myself, I can tell you firsthand it doesn't write award winning prose. It is a structural thinker applied to a domain that has structure.

The story, characters, and themes must be yours. Claude does not generate your story for you, at least not well. The underlying architecture—the arc, the act breaks, the relationship between plot and character development, the pacing logic—is the container your story pours into. A strong container built before you start writing makes the writing faster and better.

STORY STRUCTURE DEVELOPMENT SESSION:

```
I'm developing a story and I want to
work on the structure before I start
writing.
```

```
What I have: [Premise, protagonist,
central conflict, any scenes you
know exist, the emotional territory
you want the reader to experience]

What I don't have yet: [The
structural gaps]


Work with me on the structure. Do
not fill in the story for me. Ask
questions that help me find it. Push
back if you see structural problems.
Identify where the architecture is
weak.
```

*Do not fill in the story for me* is load-bearing. Claude's default in creative sessions is generative: offer ideas, suggest directions, produce options. For story structure work, that instinct is more hindrance than help. The instruction redirects it toward the structural intelligence you actually want.

## WORLD-BUILDING FOR EXTENDED CREATIVE UNIVERSES

World-building is constructing the physical, social, historical, and metaphysical rules of a fictional universe. Done well, it creates conditions where stories feel inevitable rather than invented, because every event follows from the logic of the world rather than the convenience of the plot.

It is also, for a solo creator, an enormous amount of work. The amount of detail a coherent universe requires, even if 90% of it never appears explicitly on the page, is substantial. Claude is a genuine force multiplier here because it can hold and extend a world's internal logic across sessions in ways that would otherwise require a dedicated collaborator or a reference document the size of a small novel.

George R.R. Martin has spoken extensively on universe building, and if he had Claude at his disposal in the 1990s, we'd almost certainly have a complete *Song of Ice and Fire* by now.

### The Construction Phase

Construction is building the world from the raw material of your creative vision: the central concept, the rules you know you want, the tone and feeling of the universe, the questions the world is designed to explore. Claude's job is to develop the implications of what you've established and identify the gaps in the architecture.

```
WORLD-BUILDING CONSTRUCTION SESSION:

I'm building a fictional universe. Here's what I know:

Core concept: [The central premise]

Tone and feeling: [What the world feels like to inhabit]

Rules I know exist: [Physical laws, social structures, history, anything decided]

Central tensions: [The conflicts built into the world that generate stories]

Ask me questions that surface the implications of what I've established. Point out where my rules create contradictions. Help me find the details that make this world feel inhabited rather than invented.
```

### The Consistency Phase

Once the world has substance, the consistency phase uses Claude as a continuity checker. You load the world-building document at the start of each session and ask Claude to flag anything in new material that violates the established rules.

CONSISTENCY CHECKING SESSION:

```
Here is the world-building document for [UNIVERSE NAME]: [PASTE]

I'm going to share a scene I've written. Read it against the world-building document. Does anything contradict the established rules? Does anything feel inconsistent with the tone or logic we've established? Flag everything, even small things.
```

Continuity errors in world-building are expensive to fix late and cheap to prevent early. Claude holding the full world document in context while evaluating new material catches what a creator who is too immersed in the work cannot see.

> *The best creative universes feel like they existed before the stories did. Claude helps you build the world deeply enough that the*

> *stories feel like discovery rather than invention.*

## SOCIAL CONTENT CALENDARS AT CREATIVE SCALE

Social content is a creative problem that most people treat as a mechanical one. They think about volume, frequency, and platform requirements. They end up with content that checks those boxes and does nothing else. The accounts that build real audiences treat social content as an extension of their own creative mind. Intentionally or not, they create a body of work with a consistent voice, a developing point of view, and a relationship with the audience that compounds over time.

Skip the calendar and go straight to creating your content philosophy. What is this account actually for, what is it building toward, what should the audience feel after encountering it consistently over months? That philosophy is the brief every piece of content gets measured against.

### CONTENT PHILOSOPHY SESSION:

```
I want to develop a content philosophy for [ACCOUNT/BRAND] before I build a content calendar.
```

```
What the account is currently:
[Honest description]

What I want it to become: [The
audience, reputation, feeling of
encountering this account]

What I believe that most accounts in
this space don't say: [Your genuine
point of view]

Help me develop a content
philosophy: a statement of what this
account is for, what it stands for,
and what principles should govern
every piece of content it produces.
```

Once the philosophy exists, the calendar session is grounded in something real. You are generating ideas that express a coherent point of view, and Claude can evaluate each one against what you established instead of creating content that will get lost in a void.

CALENDAR DEVELOPMENT SESSION:

```
Content philosophy: [PASTE]

Brand brief: [PASTE]
```

```
I need a [X]-post content plan for [PLATFORM] covering [TIME PERIOD]. For each post: the core idea in one sentence, the format, and a draft caption or opening line.

Every post should be something we'd actually be proud to publish. No filler. If you can't reach [X] posts that meet that standard, give me fewer and tell me where the gaps are.
```

That last instruction changes the output from a list of ideas with variable quality to a set that has been held to a standard. Claude will sometimes come back with 22 strong ideas and flag half of them as weak. That is more useful than 30 ideas presented as equally valid.

## THE CREATIVE CONSTRAINT AS A TOOL

One pattern runs through every application in this chapter and is worth naming before we close.

The most productive sessions are the ones where Claude is given specific constraints, not open-ended creative latitude. The screenplay concept session constrains Claude to questioning rather than writing.

The story structure session constrains it to structure rather than story. The world-building session constrains it to developing the implications of your rules rather than inventing its own. The content calendar session constrains it to a philosophy rather than generic generation.

Creativity is best harnessed when it is put inside the chosen constraints of a box. The box defines the problem clearly enough that real solutions become possible.

Design the constraints. Build within them. Everything worth making and enjoying gets made that way.

# CHAPTER ELEVEN

## Claude for Strategic Thinking

*How to use AI as a sparring partner for the decisions that actually matter*

Strategic thinking is the work most founders do worst and need most. Not because founders are bad thinkers, but because strategic thinking requires something that is genuinely hard to do alone: holding your own position firmly enough to develop it while staying loose enough to test it.

When you are the only person in the room, nobody pushes back. Nobody finds the flaw in the logic you just spent an hour building. Nobody asks the question you have been avoiding because the answer might mean rethinking something you already committed to. The echo chamber is the default condition of solo operators, and it produces decisions that feel solid until reality weighs in.

Claude changes this by having information you don't. By being genuinely willing to push back, steelman the opposing position, and find the assumptions your reasoning rests on and ask whether they actually hold. That willingness, applied consistently to the decisions that matter, is one of the most valuable things Claude offers a founder.

This chapter covers how to structure that application: the devil's advocate session, the strategy stress-test, investor strategy, pricing, competitive positioning, and how to know when Claude's input is actually useful versus when your own judgment needs to overrule it.

## THE SPARRING PARTNER MINDSET

Don't treat Claude as a consultant. It does not have a stake in your outcomes, does not know your industry the way a real domain expert does, and does not have the pattern recognition that comes from personally making and surviving a hundred decisions like the one you're facing. If you expect consultant-quality strategic advice from Claude, then expect to be typing out numerous sad face emojis in response.

What Claude is, and what it does exceptionally well, is act as a sparring partner. A sparring partner's job is to test your thinking, help you find the holes in your game, and allow you a safe space to refine your strategy. It will help you find the weak spots before you walk into the room where weak spots have consequences.

That framing changes how you set up strategic sessions. You are asking Claude to help you think more clearly about what you are already inclined to do, not simply what to do. Your thinking gets sharper, and the decision stays yours.

## THE DEVIL'S ADVOCATE SESSION

The devil's advocate session is the foundational strategic use of Claude and the most commonly misused one. Most people describe their position, ask Claude to argue against it, and get back a polite list of generic counterarguments that do not threaten anything.

The generic counterargument problem is a setup problem. Claude defaults to the kinds of counterarguments that apply broadly to decisions of this type, which are often not the ones that matter for your particular situation.

Fix it by giving Claude more than your position. Give it the reasoning, the assumptions the reasoning rests on, and the evidence you used to reach your conclusion. The deeper the setup, the more targeted the pushback.

DEVIL'S ADVOCATE SESSION SETUP:

```
I want you to argue against a decision I'm leaning toward. Your job is not to be politely skeptical. Your job is to find the strongest possible case against this, including arguments I may not have considered and assumptions I may not have examined.

The decision: [STATE IT CLEARLY]

My reasoning: [Explain why you think this is right, in full]

The assumptions this reasoning rests on: [What has to be true for your reasoning to hold]

Evidence I'm using: [What you've observed or concluded that supports this]

What I'm most uncertain about: [The parts you're least confident in]

Now argue against it. Be thorough. Be specific to my situation. Do not pull punches.
```

What comes back from a well-set-up session is different in kind from what comes back from a generic one. Claude will find the assumption doing the most work that is least examined. It will identify the scenario where your evidence points the other direction. It will take the thing you listed as an uncertainty and explain why your uncertainty is warranted.

The goal is to test your argument in AI court. Most of the time you will come out with stronger conviction, not less, because the reasoning held under pressure. But occasionally Claude surfaces something that genuinely changes your view. Those occasions are worth every session that ends in confirmation.

> *The decision that survives a well-constructed devil's advocate session is one you can defend to anyone. The decision that doesn't survive it is one you needed to reconsider before it was too late.*

## STRESS-TESTING A STRATEGY

Where the devil's advocate session tests a single decision, the strategy stress-test examines an entire direction: a go-to-market approach, a channel strategy, a partnership model, a product roadmap. The goal is to hammer out the scenarios in which a set of decisions could actually fail.

Scenario planning is a discipline large organizations do formally and solo founders almost never do at all. Claude makes it practical at the founder scale.

STRATEGY STRESS-TEST SESSION:

```
I want to stress-test a strategy before I commit resources to it.

The strategy: [What you're doing, the sequence, the resource commitments, the expected outcomes]

Context: [Market conditions, competitive landscape, your current position, constraints]

Run three scenarios:

Scenario 1: The strategy works as planned. What conditions need to be true for this to happen? What are
```

```
the two or three things most likely
to go wrong even in a success
scenario?

Scenario 2: The strategy fails. What
is the most likely failure mode and
how does it unfold? Be specific
about where in the sequence things
go wrong and why.

Scenario 3: The environment changes
in a way I haven't anticipated. What
external shift would most threaten
this strategy, and what would that
look like in practice?

After the three scenarios: what is
the single most important thing I
should monitor to know early whether
this strategy is on track or off it?
```

That last question is the one most strategy sessions never get to. An early warning indicator, the thing you watch that tells you before the consequences are obvious whether the strategy is working, is as valuable as the plan itself. Most strategic documents end at the plan. This session does not.

## INVESTOR STRATEGY

Investor strategy is one of the highest-stakes strategic domains a founder navigates, and the one with the sharpest information asymmetry. Investors have seen hundreds of deals. Most founders have navigated one or two. That gap means founders are a walking example of the Dunning-Krueger effect. This is precisely where Claude's devil's advocate capability earns its keep.

### Preparation: Knowing Your Weaknesses Before They Do

Before any investor conversation, find your own vulnerabilities first then think through them carefully enough that you can address them directly rather than getting caught off guard.

INVESTOR PREPARATION SESSION:

```
I'm preparing for a conversation
with an investor who focuses on
[CATEGORY/STAGE]. Play the role of a
skeptical, experienced investor who
has seen a hundred pitches like
mine.

Here is my business: [KEY METRICS,
MODEL, STAGE, TRACTION]
```

```
Ask me the hardest questions this
investor is likely to ask. Focus
especially on where my numbers or
story are weakest. After I answer
each question, tell me whether my
answer would satisfy a genuinely
skeptical investor and what I should
add or change.
```

This session works best as a genuine back-and-forth. Claude asks a question, you answer, Claude evaluates the answer and pushes further if it is not satisfying. By the end you will have found the three or four questions your current answers do not handle well, with time left to develop better ones before the stakes are real.

### Positioning: What Kind of Investor, and Why

Not all capital is the same. The investor strategy question is not just how to raise but from whom and on what terms. Claude is useful for thinking through the positioning question before outreach begins.

INVESTOR POSITIONING SESSION:

```
I'm thinking through my investor
strategy and want to make sure I'm
```

```
targeting the right type of capital
before I start outreach.

The business: [Brief overview]

What I need the capital for:
[Specific use of funds]

My current thinking on investor
type: [Angels, family offices,
strategic, institutional, etc.]

Challenge my thinking. What type of
investor is actually best aligned
with what I'm building? What are the
hidden costs of the type I'm
currently targeting? Are there types
I'm not considering that would be a
better fit?
```

An investor who gives you their money and wants nothing to do with the day to day operations is far different from one who becomes a business version of your mom. Know which one you want and why before sending out a single email, proposal, or pitch deck.

## PRICING STRATEGY

Pricing is one of the most consequential strategic decisions a founder makes and one of the most commonly made on thin thinking. Most founders price on cost-plus instinct, loosely informed by what competitors charge, without working through what their price position actually signals or who it attracts.

Claude is useful for pricing not because it knows your market better than you do, but because it surfaces the dimensions of the decision that are easy to overlook when you're focused on the number itself.

PRICING STRATEGY SESSION:

```
I want to think through the pricing strategy for [PRODUCT/SERVICE]. I have a number in mind but want to pressure-test the thinking before I commit.


The product: [What it is, what it does, who it's for]

The number I'm considering: [Price point and structure]

My reasoning: [Why this number]

Competitive context: [What alternatives exist and what they charge]
```

```
Examine four dimensions of this
decision:

1. What does this price signal about
the brand, and is that signal
consistent with the positioning?

2. What customer does it attract,
and is that the customer I want?

3. What is the strategic cost of
pricing here versus higher or lower?

4. What would have to be true about
the market for this price to be
wrong?
```

The fourth question is the one most founders skip and most need. Pricing decisions live for a long time. Knowing the conditions under which your current price is wrong tells you what to watch for as the market develops.

## COMPETITIVE POSITIONING

Competitive positioning is the strategic question of where you choose to compete and how you choose to be different from the alternatives your customers have. It differs from brand positioning, which is about perception, as it is more so about the structural choices that make your position defensible.

The most useful thing Claude can do here is map the competitive landscape from your customer's perspective rather than your own. Founders see the landscape in terms of companies and products. Customers see it in terms of jobs to be done and the full set of alternatives available to accomplish those jobs. Those maps look different. The customer's map is usually more strategically useful.

COMPETITIVE POSITIONING SESSION:

```
I want to map the competitive landscape for [BRAND/PRODUCT] from the customer's perspective.


The customer I most want to reach: [Specific description]

The job they are hiring my product to do: [What problem they are solving]

The full set of alternatives they have: [Not just direct competitors but everything they could do instead, including nothing]


Map the landscape. Where is the least contested space? Where am I currently positioned and is that where I want to be? What would it
```

```
take to occupy the position I
actually want, and what would I have
to give up to get there?
```

## WHEN TO OVERRIDE CLAUDE'S STRATEGIC INPUT

This chapter has made a strong case for Claude as a strategic sparring partner, but there are specific situations where your own judgment should overrule what Claude produces.

The first is when Claude's input is based on pattern rather than context. Claude has well-developed pattern responses to common strategic scenarios. Those patterns are useful starting points, but are not always applicable to your specific situation, and the ways your situation differs from the pattern are often the most strategically important facts. When Claude's advice sounds like advice for any company in your category, it probably is. Push deeper into your specific context before accepting it.

The second is when the decision involves relationships, culture, or values Claude cannot fully weigh. Strategic decisions are made inside specific relationships with specific people, within a specific culture you are building, and against values you have decided are non-negotiable. Claude does not know those things the way you do. Decisions that turn on them require your judgment more than Claude's analysis.

The third is when your instinct is strong and Claude's counterargument is technically valid but missing something real. Claude argues from logic and evidence. Sometimes the right call has a quality that cannot be fully articulated in logic and evidence, a sense of rightness that comes from deep familiarity with your market, your customers, or yourself. Examine the instinct. If it holds, trust it.

Claude sharpens your thinking, but it’s your thinking that drives the decision. That division of labor is the right one.

PART THREE: USE CASES THAT ACTUALLY MATTER

# CHAPTER TWELVE

## Claude for Writing That Has a Point of View

*Political commentary, essays, persuasive content, and thought leadership that actually says something*

Most writing has a topic, covers that topic from multiple angles, hedges where controversy might arise, lands somewhere safely moderate, and produces the kind of content that nobody disagrees with because nobody cares enough to react to it at all.

Writing with a point of view is different. It takes a position, argues for something, and is willing to be wrong about that something in order to be interesting about it. It treats the reader as an adult who can evaluate an argument rather than a consumer who needs to be soothed. It is the kind of writing that gets shared, remembered, and argued about at dinner tables.

It is also the kind of writing that is nearly impossible to produce with AI. AI is trained to be helpful, harmless, your sycophantic best friend. It has a gravitational pull toward the balanced, the hedged, and the uncontroversial. Left to its defaults, Claude produces writing that is technically competent and editorially spineless. It presents both sides. It acknowledges complexity. It concludes with something everyone can nod along to.

Boring!

But with the right setup, Claude can produce writing that is genuinely argued, genuinely positioned, and genuinely worth reading. This chapter is about how to get there, using political commentary, essay writing, persuasive content, and thought leadership as the four primary applications. By the end you'll have Claude spitting out biting satirical editorials or highfalutin thinkpieces, whichever most strikes your particular writing fancy.

## WHY CLAUDE HEDGES AND HOW TO STOP IT

Claude was trained to be helpful to a wide range of people with a wide range of views. Writing that takes strong positions risks being unhelpful to the people who hold the opposing position. The training reflects that concern, and the result is a model with a gravitational pull toward the center on any topic where reasonable people disagree.

This is appropriate for some purposes, but for opinionated writing, it's actively counterproductive. An essay that presents both sides is not an essay. Commentary that acknowledges the merits of every position is not commentary. Thought leadership that hedges every claim is the equivalent of a jungle cat pissing on every tree in the area then rolling over the first time he's challenged.

The solution is to establish clearly and early that the writing task requires a committed point of view, that you are providing that point of view, and that Claude's job is to argue it as compellingly as possible rather than moderate it into mush.

POINT-OF-VIEW ESTABLISHMENT PROMPT:

```
I'm writing a piece that takes a strong position on [TOPIC]. The position is: [STATE IT WITHOUT HEDGING].

I am asking you to argue this position as compellingly as possible using the strongest available evidence and sharpest available logic.
```

```
If the argument has a genuine
weakness that would undermine its
credibility with a serious reader,
flag it before we draft. Otherwise,
commit to the position and argue it
to the fullest extent.
```

That last instruction draws a line between weaknesses that need to be addressed to make the argument credible and weaknesses Claude would insert purely as a hedge. You want the former flagged. You do not want the latter showing up in the piece as a rhetorical disclaimer that softens the landing.

## POLITICAL COMMENTARY

Political commentary interprets political events, developments, or figures from a defined perspective and draws conclusions a reader can argue with or be persuaded by. It is distinct from political reporting, which describes what happened, and from political analysis, which explains why. Commentary says what it means, what should be done about it, and ideally does it in a compelling way that inspires readers to action.

Good political commentary requires three things Claude can help develop but cannot supply: a coherent political worldview, genuine knowledge of the subject matter, and a voice readers recognize as belonging to someone with real convictions. The worldview and the knowledge are yours. The voice, as covered in Chapter Seven, can be developed and held across sessions with the persona lock. What Claude adds is the structural discipline to turn your convictions and knowledge into arguments that hold together against scrutiny.

### The Argument Architecture Session

Build the argument architecture before drafting. This forces you to identify the core claim, the supporting evidence, the strongest objection, and your answer to it. Doing this work before writing prevents the most common failure in political writing: pieces that make a claim in the first paragraph and then meander for the next eight.

ARGUMENT ARCHITECTURE SESSION:

```
I'm writing commentary on [TOPIC].
Before we draft, I want to build the
argument architecture.


Core claim: [The one sentence this
piece argues]
```

```
Supporting evidence: [Facts, examples, or logic that support the claim]

Strongest objection a serious critic would make: [State it fairly]

My answer to that objection: [How the argument survives the best challenge]


Evaluate this architecture. Is the core claim actually arguable, or is it either too obvious or too extreme? Is my evidence sufficient for the claim I'm making? Is my answer to the objection genuinely satisfying or am I dodging? Tell me where the architecture is weak before we build on it.
```

The evaluation step does real work. Claude will identify where the evidence does not fully support the claim, where the objection is stronger than your answer to it, or where the core claim is so broad it cannot be argued in a single piece. Fix these before drafting, not during.

### Drafting in Voice

Once the architecture is sound, drafting follows the same voice process from Chapter Seven. Load the persona lock, share the architecture as the structural brief, and let Claude draft within those parameters.

The refinement pass for political commentary has one additional consideration: the tone of conviction. Political writing that sounds angry is unpersuasive to everyone who does not already agree. Writing that sounds detached is unserious to everyone who cares about the subject. The register to aim for is genuine conviction without performance: someone who believes what they are saying and trusts the argument to carry the persuasion.

TONE REFINEMENT PROMPT:

```
This draft is making the argument correctly but the tone is slightly off. It reads as [too strident / too detached / too academic / too rhetorical]. I want it to read as someone who believes this deeply and is making the case to a reader who is skeptical but persuadable. Adjust the tone without changing the argument.
```

## ESSAY WRITING

The essay is one of the oldest and most flexible forms of written argument. At its best, it is thinking made visible: the writer working through a problem in public, arriving somewhere the reader could not have predicted from the opening paragraph but feels was inevitable at the close.

Essays fail in two predictable ways. The first is the thesis-and-support structure imported from academic writing: state the claim, prove it, restate it. The reader knows where they are going before they start and arrives without learning anything they could not have inferred from the first sentence.

The second failure is the opposite: an essay that meanders interestingly without arriving anywhere. The prose is engaging, but by the end, the reader cannot say what the piece was actually about.

The best essays do neither. They begin in uncertainty or observation, develop through genuine inquiry, and arrive at a conclusion that feels earned. Claude can help structure this arc without determining where it goes.

ESSAY DEVELOPMENT SESSION:

```
I want to write an essay on
[SUBJECT]. Here's where I am:
```

```
What I started thinking: [The observation or question that initiated the idea]

Where my thinking has gone: [The development and complications you've encountered]

Where I think I'm landing: [Your current sense of the conclusion, even if tentative]

What I'm still uncertain about: [The part that isn't resolved]


Help me map the arc. Not a numbered outline. A sense of the journey: where the essay begins, what it moves through, where it arrives. The uncertainty is a feature, not a problem. Help me find the structure that makes it productive rather than just unresolved.
```

*Uncertainty is a feature, not a problem* is the most important instruction in that prompt. It signals to Claude that your goal is a thinking essay, not a proof-of-thesis essay. The structure it suggests in response will be different, and better off for it.

## PERSUASIVE CONTENT AND THOUGHT LEADERSHIP

Persuasive content argues toward a specific action: buy this, believe this, do this differently. Thought leadership argues toward a specific way of seeing: here is a frame for understanding this domain that you did not have before, and it will change how you act within it.

Both require genuine conviction. Persuasive content that does not actually believe in what it is arguing is manipulation, and readers feel it without being able to name it. Thought leadership without an actual distinctive thought is content marketing with a grander title on the door.

Claude is most useful for both when the conviction already exists and the task is translating it into a form that persuades people who do not already share it.

### Mapping the Reader's Current Position

The most common failure in persuasive writing is starting from your position rather than the reader's. You know why the thing is true, but the reader doesn't necessarily share your starting premises. The gap between your starting point and theirs is where most persuasive writing loses people, not because the argument is wrong but because it assumes agreement that has not been established.

```
READER POSITION MAPPING SESSION:

I want to write a persuasive piece arguing [POSITION]. Before I draft, I want to map the reader's current position.

My target reader: [Specific description, not 'general audience']

What they currently believe about this topic: [Your honest assessment, including beliefs that conflict with your position]

What evidence or experience led them to that belief: [Why their current position makes sense from their vantage point]

What they would need to see or understand to move toward my position: [The path from where they are to where you need them to be]

Design the persuasive arc. Start where the reader is. Identify the moment in the piece where they either accept the reframe or
```

```
disengage, and tell me what has to
happen at that moment to keep them.
```

That last instruction surfaces the hinge point of any persuasive piece: the moment the reader is asked to accept a premise they did not arrive with. Every persuasive piece has one. Designing it carefully is the difference between writing that converts and writing that preaches to the choir.

### Thought Leadership That Actually Leads

Thought leadership fails when it is indistinguishable from good summary. Summarizing the current state of a domain clearly is valuable, but it is not leadership. Leadership requires a claim about where the domain is going, what is wrong with how it is currently understood, or a framework the reader should adopt that they do not currently have.

THOUGHT LEADERSHIP DEVELOPMENT SESSION:

```
I want to write a thought leadership
piece in [DOMAIN]. Here's my actual
thought: [State the idea, claim, or
reframe that is distinctively yours]
```

```
Here's why most people in this domain see it differently: [The current consensus and why it exists]

Here's why I think they're wrong or incomplete: [Your specific disagreement]

Here's what led me to this view: [What you've seen or interpreted differently]


Build the argument. The piece should make someone feel they now have a frame they did not have before. It should not summarize the domain. It should challenge something about how it is currently understood.
```

> *Thought leadership that does not actually disagree with anything is not leadership. It is content. Claude can help you argue a genuine disagreement compellingly. It cannot manufacture the disagreement for you.*

## HOW CLAUDE HANDLES NUANCE AND CONTESTED IDEAS

One of the genuine strengths of Claude for this category of writing is how it handles contested ideas. Claude will engage with arguments that are genuinely controversial, represent positions it does not hold in order to help you argue against them, and push back on your reasoning without retreating to the top of the fence when you have asked it to commit.

What it will not do is produce content that is purely inflammatory, misrepresents facts in service of a position, or argues for things outside the bounds of legitimate disagreement. Those limits exist and they are real. I know. I've tried breaking them. For the kind of writing this chapter is about, arguing from genuine conviction on contested but legitimate questions, those limits are almost never relevant.

The practical implication: do not preemptively self-censor your prompts because you assume Claude will not engage with a strong position. Load the position, establish the commitment to argue it, and let Claude engage. If it pulls its punches in a way that undermines the piece, the refinement techniques from Chapter Six are your tool for addressing that specifically.

## THE VOICE QUESTION FOR OPINIONATED WRITING

A pen name used for political commentary represents a specific political identity, a specific voice, a specific set of convictions and characteristic ways of arguing them. All of that can be captured in a persona document and held consistently across sessions.

The persona lock for a political writer contains everything the standard voice persona lock contains, with one additional layer: the political worldview itself. It doesn't list positions on individual issues, which change and evolve over time, but the underlying values and analytical framework that generate those positions. The difference between "this writer believes X about immigration" and "this writer believes individual liberty is the primary political value and analyzes all policy through that lens" is the difference between a list of opinions and a coherent worldview. The latter produces consistent, arguable writing. The former produces a collection of positions that may or may not add up to anything.

Developing a worldview document for a political writer persona is itself a productive Claude session. Bring your actual convictions and Claude helps you develop them into a coherent framework that can be applied consistently and held across many pieces of writing over time.

The views remain yours. Claude sharpens the form they take and keeps them consistent at the level of architecture, not just surface.

## WHAT MAKES THE WRITING NOT SOUND LIKE AI

The writing sounds human when the thinking behind it is human. Full stop.

Claude can produce grammatically correct, structurally sound, stylistically accomplished prose. What it cannot produce is the numerous observations that come from your specific vantage point, the anecdote drawn from your actual life, the conviction that shows in writing because the writer actually holds it rather than is performing it.

Those elements have to be inserted by you as the raw material the session is built around. The argument architecture session asks what you actually believe and what evidence you actually have. The reader position mapping asks you to genuinely consider where your reader is starting from. The thought leadership session asks you to state a real disagreement with the current consensus.

When the thinking is genuine, the writing built on it reads as genuine. The craft assistance Claude provides, the structure, the argumentation, the voice calibration, is in service of real content. Without the real content, the craft assistance produces something that reads exactly like what it is: a well-executed performance of having a point of view, by a machine that has none.

Bring the thinking. Bring the style. Claude will help you make it worth reading.

# CHAPTER THIRTEEN

## The Daily Stack

*What an AI-native workflow actually looks like for a solo operator*

Most productivity advice about AI tools focuses on individual use cases in isolation. *Here is how to use Claude for email. Here is how to use it for content. Here is how to use it for research.* Each application is explained as if it exists independently of everything else, to be pulled out when the relevant task comes up and put back when it's done.

That approach produces a novice AI user: someone who reaches for Claude occasionally, for specific tasks, when they remember it exists. The results are fine, in theory, but it's the technological equivalent of leaving an enormous amount of meat on the bone

The operators who get transformative results do not use Claude as a default collaborator woven into how they work every single day, for the right tasks at the right moments, consistently enough that the working relationship actually compounds.

This chapter is about what that looks like in practice. I will show you how Claude integrates into the actual rhythm of a working day, from the first productive session in the morning through the synthesis work at the end. Every individual's needs are different, but after reading, you'll be able to create a system that adapts to your specific desired set of outcomes.

## THE PROBLEM WITH ON-DEMAND AI USE

When Claude is a tool you reach for when stuck, the sessions you have with it are reactive. You are already frustrated, already spinning, already committed to a direction that may not be right. You bring Claude into a problem after you have been working on it long enough to have developed blind spots. You ask for help with the symptom rather than the underlying structure that led to it in the first place.

When Claude is a tool you engage with at the beginning of a task or a day rather than in the middle of a crisis, the sessions are generative. You are thinking forward instead of digging out of a hole. You are using Claude to structure your approach before you have invested in a track heading to who-knows-where.

The difference in output quality between reactive and proactive use is the difference between using Claude to rescue work and using Claude to produce better work from the start. The daily stack is built around the latter.

## THE MORNING BRIEF

The most valuable Claude session of any working day is often the first one, and it is the one most people never have: the morning brief.

Take 10-15 minutes, before doing anything else, to set up three essential components: orientation, prioritization, and preparation.

### Orientation

Orientation is a quick synthesis of where things stand. It is a spoken or written summary that forces you to articulate what is in play across your projects before you start working on any of them. The act of articulating it is useful by itself, independent of what Claude does with it.

MORNING ORIENTATION PROMPT:

```
Here's where things stand across my work this morning:


[BRAND/PROJECT 1]: [One or two sentences on current status and what needs to move today]

[BRAND/PROJECT 2]: [Same]

[INITIATIVE]: [Same]


Based on this, what are the two or three things most worth focusing on today? What dependencies or risks do you see that I should keep in mind?
```

Sometimes Claude will confirm what you already knew. But the process of writing the orientation, of forcing yourself to summarize the current state of each thing in one or two sentences, consistently surfaces the thing you have been avoiding or the dependency you have been soft-pedaling to yourself. That alone is worth the 10 minutes.

### Prioritization

If the orientation surfaces more than one day can hold, the prioritization step sequences it in an order that allows you to get your work done. Use this one prompt:

PRIORITIZATION PROMPT:

```
Given what I've shared, I have more to address than I can finish today. What is time-sensitive versus important but not urgent? What has downstream dependencies that makes it higher priority than it might appear? What can be deferred without real cost?
```

The *downstream dependency question* changes prioritization more often than you'd expect. The task that looks medium-priority in isolation is sometimes high-priority because future links in the chain are waiting on it. Claude, holding the full context of your orientation, spots those connections faster than you can when you are inside the work.

### Preparation

Preparation is valuable particularly when you have something significant coming in the day ahead, be it a meeting, a call, or a deliverable with real stakes.

PREPARATION PROMPT:

```
I have [MEETING / CALL / DELIVERABLE] today. Context: [Brief description of who, what, and why it matters]

What should I be prepared for? What is the most important thing to accomplish in this interaction? What could go wrong and how should I handle it if it does?
```

One preparation prompt before a significant interaction is worth avoiding the psychological prison stint that can ensue after one that did not go as planned.

## CONTENT BATCHING

Content batching is producing multiple pieces of content in a single focused session rather than writing each piece individually as it is needed. It is more efficient because the context-loading cost, the time spent bringing Claude up to speed on the brand, the voice, the strategic intent, gets paid once and spread across many outputs instead of paid separately every time.

For a founder managing one or more brands with ongoing content needs, content batching is one of the highest-leverage applications in the daily stack. A single two-hour session can produce a week or more of scheduled content across channels.

Load the brand brief and persona lock at the start, establish the content themes and formats, then move through the content types systematically, producing and refining each batch before moving to the next.

CONTENT BATCHING SESSION STRUCTURE:

```
We're doing a content batching session for [BRAND]. Here's what we're producing today:

- 5 Instagram posts (mix of product, brand story, and point of view)

- 2 email subject line options for this week's send

- 3 short-form video concepts with hook and structure

- 1 longer caption for a behind-the-scenes post

[PASTE BRAND BRIEF AND PERSONA LOCK]
```

```
Let's work through these in order.
Start with the Instagram posts. For
each one, give me the core idea, the
draft caption, and a note on the
visual direction. Hold the brand
voice throughout. We'll review each
batch before moving to the next.
```

*Review each batch before moving to the next* is a critical input that prevents the session from producing a large volume of content that needs extensive revision later. Refine each batch to a publishable standard before generating the next one. Volume over quality is a trap that wastes more time than it saves.

## DECISION SUPPORT THROUGHOUT THE DAY

Beyond the structured morning brief and content batching sessions, the most common daily use of Claude is decision support.

Ask it a specific question, provide the relevant context, and reap the benefits of a fast exchange that either confirms your instinct or surfaces something worth considering before you act.

### DECISION SUPPORT PROMPT PATTERN:

```
Quick decision I need to make: [One sentence]

Context: [Two or three sentences of relevant background]

My current lean: [Which way you're inclined and why]

What I'm uncertain about: [The part making you pause]


Is there anything in what I've shared that should change my thinking? What am I not considering?
```

Stating your current lean and your uncertainty does two things. It prevents Claude from simply validating whatever direction you appear to be heading without engaging with the actual question. And it focuses the response on the specific thing that needs clarification rather than a broad analysis nobody asked for.

Used consistently throughout a working day, these sessions change the character of the decisions you make. The discipline of articulating your lean and your uncertainty before acting catches the decisions where the uncertainty is higher than you realized. Claude's advice can be sound, but that pause you take to consider the situation before acting is often the most valuable part.

## END-OF-DAY SYNTHESIS

The end-of-day synthesis is the bookend to the morning brief, and it is the session most people skip because the day's work is done and cocktail hour calls. Do not, however, treat it as optional.

The end-of-day brief captures what happened in a form that can inform tomorrow's morning brief. Second, it surfaces anything unresolved, at risk, or needing to be carried forward explicitly, rather than just letting it float around in your own memory overnight.

### END-OF-DAY SYNTHESIS PROMPT:

```
Here's what happened today across my
work: [Brief summary of what you
worked on, what moved, what didn't,
any new information that came in]

What should carry forward into
tomorrow? What's unresolved that I
need to pick back up? What did
today's work surface that changes
any of my current priorities or
plans?
```

The value is not primarily what Claude produces in the session but what the act of doing it produces in you: a clean handoff from today to tomorrow, with the important things identified rather than left to drift overnight.

Founders running multiple entities find this especially valuable. The cognitive load of holding the current state of three or four active projects simultaneously is real and cumulative. The end-of-day synthesis offloads that load into a structured record. Tomorrow's morning brief starts from that record rather than from whatever managed to survive in working memory while you slept.

## WHAT A FULL DAY LOOKS LIKE

Here is a concrete picture of how these elements fit together for a solo multi-entity operator:

Morning Morning brief: orientation, prioritization, and preparation for the day's significant interactions.

Mid-morning Deep work session: highest-priority substantive work, often involving Claude for production planning, brand work, or strategic thinking.

Late morning Decision support: quick targeted sessions as operational questions arise. 5-10 minutes each, as needed.

Afternoon Content batching or communications: vendor emails, proposal drafts, or a content batch depending on the week's priorities.

Late afternoon Follow-up and loose ends: shorter tasks that accumulated during the day, many of which Claude handles quickly with context.

End of day Synthesis: review and capture.

The daily stack is about using Claude at the right moments, in the right way, consistently enough that the working relationship compounds into something that looks, from the outside, like an unfair advantage. Because, quite frankly, when used in this way it is an extremely unfair advantage.

## BUILDING THE HABIT, NOT THE SYSTEM

The founders who sustain a productive AI workflow are not the ones who build an elaborate system and enforce it on themselves. They are the ones who internalize two or three consistent practices and build out from there as the habit develops. The morning brief and content batching are the two I would prioritize.

Start with the morning brief. Do it every working day for two weeks. Do not worry about whether you are doing it perfectly. The practice itself will teach you how to do it well, and what you learn will shape the rest of how you integrate Claude into your work.

14 consecutive days of using a morning brief is a habit, and a habit is worth more than any system you could possibly build.

PART FOUR: BUILDING YOUR AI WORKFLOW

# CHAPTER FOURTEEN

## Claude and Your Other Tools

*How Claude fits into a broader stack, and how to make the connections that multiply its value*

Claude is the center of gravity in the workflow described in this book. You have a publishing stack, a design stack, a scheduling system, social platforms, and a communication layer. Claude lives alongside all of it, and the question is how to do it in a way that makes each one more useful as opposed to just more complicated.

I want to make the answer as concrete as possible by giving you a practical look at how Claude connects to the specific tools that show up most often in the daily working life of a solo multi-entity operator. Story universe building tools, design tools, publishing workflows, communication tools, and social scheduling each have a specific connection point that is worth knowing before you sit down to work.

Claude is most powerful when the outputs of your other tools flow into it as context, and when Claude's outputs flow back into those tools as inputs, the seams between applications disappear and the work moves faster. That is the goal, a cohesive team that equates to greater than the sum of its parts.

## THE CONNECTIVE TISSUE MODEL

Think of Claude as the hub that connects everything else in your stack. Your project management tool knows what tasks exist. Your communication tool knows what was said. Your design tool knows what the brand looks like. None of them talk to each other.

The way you build that connection is simple: before asking Claude to do anything, bring the relevant outputs from your other tools into the Claude session as context. Paste in the task list, drop in the brief, share the notes from the call, and Claude will combine all of them into one cohesive output that operates synergistically and effectively.

## CLAUDE AND SCREENWRITING AND STORY UNIVERSE TOOLS

Screenwriting software handles formatting beautifully. World-building tools handle reference databases, whether via a wiki, a notes system, or a sprawling folder of documents. Neither one helps you figure out what your story actually is before you start filling them up. That is where Claude earns its place in the creative workflow: upstream of both, doing the conceptual and structural work that makes everything that happens inside them faster and more intentional.

For screenwriting, use Claude to develop the log line, build the beat sheet, identify structural problems before they get baked into 50 pages of draft, and work through the subtext of a scene before writing the dialogue. The screenplay software is where the final output lives. Claude helps you build the architecture that captivates your future audience.

PRE-WRITING ARCHITECTURE SESSION:

```
Before I open my screenwriting
software, I want to make sure the
structure is sound.


Here is where I am: [Premise, what I
know exists in the story, what I
haven't figured out yet]


I want to identify the structural
problems now rather than discover
them in the rewrite. What is weak in
```

```
this architecture? Where is the
protagonist passive when they should
be driving the story? Where do the
stakes feel unearned? Tell me what
to fix before I start writing pages.
Identify any other potential
weaknesses you notice.
```

For story universe development, whether that is a fictional IP, a world-building project, or a creative universe that spans multiple formats and properties, Claude's role is both construction and continuity.

In the construction phase, you are developing the rules of the world, its history, its tensions, the logic that makes stories set inside it feel inevitable rather than invented. How do the Lannisters relate to the Baratheons? What is the historical context that keeps Westeros and Easteros so dynamically different from each other? Claude asks the questions that surface implications you had not considered and flags contradictions in the architecture before they compound.

In the continuity phase, the world-building document you have built becomes the reference Claude holds in context while evaluating new material. Every scene, every character decision, every plot development gets checked against the established rules of the universe before it gets written into the draft. Robb Stark was married before the events of the story took place, so why is he taking a bride in Act 2 while on a military campaign. Continuity errors are cheap to fix at the outline stage and expensive to fix when you're printing out drafts. Claude as a continuity partner changes that math considerably.

STORY UNIVERSE CONTINUITY SESSION:

```
Here is the world-building document
for [UNIVERSE NAME]: [PASTE]


I'm going to share a scene I've
written for this universe. Read it
against the world-building document.
Does anything contradict the
established rules? Does anything
feel inconsistent with the tone or
logic we've built? Does this scene
add something to the universe or
does it just use it as a backdrop?
Flag everything, including small
things.
```

The thread connecting both of these applications is the same one that runs through this entire chapter. Claude sits upstream of your creativity, doing the conceptual and structural work that makes everything you build more intentional and more coherent.

## CLAUDE AND DESIGN TOOLS

Claude produces language while design tools produce visual outputs.. The connection runs in both directions, and both directions are worth understanding.

From design to Claude: when you have visual brand assets, one of the most valuable things Claude can do is help you develop the language that corresponds to them. A logo, a color palette, a set of brand photographs carry an implicit voice, a set of associations and feelings and positions that the visual choices express. Articulating that implicit voice in language is both a useful brand exercise and a prerequisite for any copy that needs to feel visually consistent with what the brand actually looks like.

VISUAL-TO-LANGUAGE SESSION:

```
I'm going to upload images that display the visual identity of [BRAND] and I want you to help me develop the language that corresponds to it.
```

```
What associations does this visual identity create? What does a brand that looks like this sound like when it writes? What words, sentence structures, and tonal qualities are consistent with these visual choices, and which ones would feel like a mismatch?
```

The brand briefs, voice guides, and positioning documents that Claude helps you develop are the inputs that produce better visual work. A designer working from a Claude-developed mythology document has a fundamentally different creative brief than one working from the instruction to “make it look premium”. The language work Claude helps you develop becomes portable enough to carry into every other part of the brand, including the visual decisions.

There is a third connection point that most people overlook entirely: using Claude to write prompts for AI image generators. Tools like Midjourney, DALL-E, Firefly, and Ideogram are only as good as the prompts you feed them, and most people feed them something like "create a product photo of a hot sauce bottle on a wooden table." What comes back is exactly that: a generic, flat, forgettable image of a hot sauce bottle on a wooden table.

Claude understands visual language in a way that most founders do not have the vocabulary for. It can direct lighting, depth of field, color grading, compositional style, photographic references, mood and atmosphere. Give Claude your brand brief and a description of the image you need, and ask it to write the generation prompt. What it produces will be specific enough that the image generator actually has something to work with.

```
IMAGE GENERATION PROMPT SESSION:

I need to generate an image for [PURPOSE: product shot / social post / website hero / campaign creative].

Brand brief: [PASTE]

What I'm trying to convey: [The feeling, story, or message the image should communicate]

What I don't want: [Generic stock photo energy, specific things to avoid]
```

```
Write me three generation prompts for [TOOL: Midjourney / DALL-E / Firefly / etc.] that would produce images consistent with this brand and this brief. Make each prompt as specific as possible about lighting, composition, color palette, mood, and style. Then tell me which of the three is most likely to produce something usable and why.
```

The ask for three variations is deliberate. Image generation is probabilistic, and having three well-constructed prompts to run gives you a much better chance of landing something useful than running one prompt five times hoping it eventually works. The explanation of which prompt is strongest also teaches you how to write better generation prompts yourself over time, which is worth more than any single image output.

## CLAUDE AND PUBLISHING WORKFLOWS

For anyone producing written content at scale, the publishing workflow is a sequence of stages: ideation, drafting, editing, formatting, distribution. Claude is useful at every stage, but the connections between stages are where the most efficiency is created, and where most people leave the most value on the table.

### Ideation to Draft

The connection between ideation and drafting is where most publishing workflows spring a leak. Ideas get generated in one context, notes accumulate somewhere else, and the actual drafting session starts from scratch because the ideation output was never properly translated into a drafting brief.

Claude closes this gap. Whatever came out of your ideation session, whether it was a Claude session or a personal brainstorm or a conversation, gets fed into a briefing session that translates it into the structured context a drafting session needs: the argument architecture, the intended audience, the target length, the voice parameters. The drafting session then starts with everything already in place.

### Draft to Edit

Before a draft goes to a human editor, running it through a Claude edit session catches the structural problems, voice inconsistencies, and argument gaps that are expensive for a human editor to address and cheap for Claude to flag.

PRE-EDIT CLAUDE SESSION:

```
Here is a draft of [PIECE]: [PASTE]

Before this goes to a human editor, evaluate it at the structural level. Look for three things: places where the argument loses coherence, places where the voice drifts from the established standard, and places where the reader is likely to disengage. Flag everything you find with specific locations and brief explanations. Do not rewrite. Just flag.
```

What comes back is a list of specific issues you can address before the human edit, which makes that edit faster and more focused on the things that actually require human judgment. It also makes the human editor's job more pleasant, which is worth something if you are paying them by the hour and want them to willingly take on a job with you again.

**Content to Distribution**

A finished long-form piece contains the raw material for multiple distribution formats: social posts drawn from its best lines, an email subject line that captures its hook, a short summary for a newsletter preview, a pull quote for visual content. Extracting all of these manually from a finished piece is tedious enough that most people either skip it or do it halfway. Claude handles it in a single session.

```
CONTENT ATOMIZATION SESSION:

Here is a finished piece: [PASTE]


From this piece, extract:

- 3 Instagram captions (different angles, each under 150 words)

- 5 potential social post hooks (single sentences that could stand alone)

- 2 email subject line options

- 1 short summary under 60 words for newsletter preview

- The single best pull quote from the piece


Hold the brand voice throughout. Extract and adapt what is already there. Do not write new content.
```

*Do not write new content* is essential. Without it, Claude will sometimes generate material that sounds like the piece but is not drawn from it. The distribution assets should represent the actual piece, not a Claude interpretation of what the piece was trying to say.

## CLAUDE AND COMMUNICATION TOOLS

Email and messaging tools are where a significant portion of every operator's working day disappears. Claude's role here is not to write all your communication, which would produce a communication style indistinguishable from anyone else using Claude for the same purpose, but to handle the communication that requires structure or sensitivity rather than personal spontaneity.

The communication tasks that benefit most from Claude involvement are the ones where the stakes are high and a little distance from the emotion is an asset: vendor negotiations, partnership outreach, difficult client situations, formal proposals. These are the situations covered in Chapter Nine, and the principle there applies here in full. Bring the relational context, not just the transactional ask.

The communication tasks that benefit least are the ones that depend on personal relationship and genuine spontaneity, like a quick reply to a close collaborator, a response in a context where the recipient knows exactly what you sound like and would notice immediately if something felt off, a message that is valuable precisely because it was not carefully composed.

Knowing which category a given communication falls into is itself a skill, and it is one worth developing. Not every email benefits from a Claude session. The ones that do benefit substantially, and getting that distinction right is what separates the operators who use Claude well for communication from the ones who use it for everything and slowly lose their own voice in the process.

## CLAUDE AND SOCIAL SCHEDULING TOOLS

Social scheduling tools handle the logistics of when content goes out. Claude handles what the content is and whether it is worth putting out. The connection between them is the content batching workflow from Chapter Thirteen, and it is one of the cleanest tool integrations in the entire stack.

The practical flow is straightforward: content batching sessions in Claude produce a set of approved, on-brand posts that move directly into your scheduling tool. The scheduling tool handles frequency, timing, and platform-specific requirements. Claude handles quality, voice, and strategic coherence. Neither one tries to do the other's job.

After a batch has been drafted and refined in Claude, reviewing the full set together catches a problem that reviewing posts individually misses: the set-level view. Five posts that are individually solid can collectively feel repetitive, tonally inconsistent, or unbalanced in topic distribution in ways that only become apparent when you see them side by side.

SET-LEVEL REVIEW PROMPT:

```
Here are the [X] posts we developed
in this session: [LIST THEM]

Review them as a set, not
individually. Is there appropriate
variety in topic, format, and tone?
Does any post feel redundant with
another? Is there a post that feels
significantly weaker than the others
and should be replaced? Does the set
```

```
as a whole represent the brand the
way we want?
```

## THE INTEGRATION PRINCIPLE

Every tool connection described in this chapter follows the same underlying principle, and it is worth stating directly before we close.

Claude's value multiplies when it has more context. Every connection you build between Claude and your other tools is a context connection: a way of bringing more of the relevant information into Claude before asking it to do something with that information. The screenplay writing session is better because the story universe, character relationships, and plot points are cohesive. The design brief is better because the brand mythology session developed the worldview. The distribution assets are better because the full finished piece is present rather than a summary of it.

Build the connections that bring the right context into Claude at the right moments, and the compounding follows automatically.

> *Claude is the most powerful tool in your stack when it operates as the thinking layer that connects everything else. Build the connections. The compounding follows.*

The next chapter is the honest one. What Claude cannot do, why knowing that matters as much as knowing what it can, and how to build a workflow that plays to the strengths and protects against the failures.

# CHAPTER FIFTEEN

## What Claude Can't Do

*And why knowing that is as important as knowing what it can*

This book has made a sustained case for Claude as a transformative tool for founders, operators, and creators who know how to use it. Everything described in the previous fourteen chapters works. I use it myself, under real conditions, with real stakes attached to the outcomes.

But Claude has real limitations that will cost you something real if you do not understand them before they show up. The founders who get the most out of Claude are not the ones who understand them well enough to build workflows that play to its strengths and protect against the failures.

This chapter is about what Claude does poorly, why it does it poorly, and what you do about it. Some of these limitations are technical. Some are structural. Some are inherent to what AI is and will remain regardless of how the technology advances. All of them are worth knowing now rather than learning the hard way later.

## HALLUCINATION: THE CONFIDENT WRONG ANSWER

Hallucination is the term the AI field uses for a model producing information that is false, fabricated, or confused, stated with the same confidence it uses for information that is true. It is the most consequential limitation of large language models and the one that causes the most damage when users do not understand it.

Claude hallucinates. Less than some models, more than others, but enough that treating any factual claim Claude makes as verified without checking it is a mistake you will eventually regret. Especially for specific facts: statistics, dates, quotes, citations, legal or regulatory details, technical specifications, and anything that requires precise knowledge of a particular domain.

Understanding why it happens makes it easier to anticipate when it is most likely to occur. Claude was trained on text, and it learned to produce text that is plausible and well-structured. Plausible and true are not the same thing. When Claude does not know something precisely, it produces what is statistically likely to be true given the pattern of the surrounding text. That production is fluent, confident, and sometimes completely wrong. The four situations where you should be most skeptical are these:

### Specific numerical claims

Statistics, percentages, market sizes, and financial figures that Claude cites with apparent precision should be verified independently. Claude has a strong tendency to produce specific-sounding numbers that are approximate at best and invented at worst. The more specific the number, the more skeptical you should be.

### Citations and sources

Claude will sometimes cite sources that do not exist or attribute quotes to people who never said them. This is perhaps the most dangerous form of hallucination for anyone using Claude for research or for written work that will be published. Do not publish a citation without verifying that the source exists and says what Claude says it says. This is not optional.

### Recent events

Claude has a knowledge cutoff. Events, developments, and changes that occurred after that cutoff are not in its training data. When you ask Claude about something that may have changed recently, it will either tell you it does not know, which is the honest response, or it will produce an answer based on what was true as of its training, which may no longer be accurate. For anything time-sensitive, verify independently before acting on it.

### Specialized technical or legal domains

Claude has broad knowledge but shallow expertise in highly specialized domains. Medical, legal, financial, and technical questions that require precision and current expertise are domains where Claude's responses should be treated as starting points for further research, not conclusions you act on. Claude can help you understand the landscape of a specialized question. It cannot replace a domain expert, and it will not always tell you when it is out of its depth.

The practical protocol is to calibrate your verification effort to the stakes. For creative work and ideation, where precision is not the point, proceed without verification. For factual claims that will appear in published work, be shared with investors, or inform important decisions, verify every specific claim independently before relying on it. The 10 minutes you spend checking is cheap compared to the cost of getting it wrong.

> *Claude is exceptionally good at reasoning and structure. It is unreliable for precise factual recall. Build your workflow to use the former and verify the latter. That division of labor works. Ignoring it does not.*

## NO REAL-TIME INFORMATION

Claude does not have access to the internet by default. It cannot browse, cannot check current prices, cannot read today's news, cannot look up a company's current leadership, cannot verify whether a business is still operating. Its knowledge is static, bounded by the training cutoff, and it cannot update itself with new information between your sessions.

This shapes what Claude is and is not useful for in a very practical way. It is not useful for anything that requires current information as an input: market research that needs current data, competitive analysis that needs recent developments, due diligence that needs current financials, any question where the answer depends on something that may have changed since training.

Some versions of Claude have web search capability enabled, which addresses this partially. If you have access to that capability, use it for time-sensitive queries. If you do not, the workaround is straightforward: do the information gathering yourself in the tool built for it, then bring what you found into Claude as context for the analysis you need.

> COMPENSATING FOR THE REAL-TIME LIMITATION:
>
> `I've gathered the following current information about [TOPIC]: [PASTE WHAT YOU FOUND]`
>
> `Using this as the factual foundation, help me [ANALYSIS TASK]. Do not draw on any information about this topic that predates what I've provided here, as the situation may have changed.`

That last instruction matters more than it might seem. Without it, Claude will sometimes blend the current information you provided with older training data, producing a response that mixes accurate current facts with outdated ones in ways that are genuinely difficult to untangle. The instruction to treat your provided information as the authoritative source prevents that blending and keeps the analysis clean.

## MEMORY BETWEEN SESSIONS

Claude does not remember previous sessions. Every conversation begins fresh, with no access to what was discussed, decided, or produced in earlier exchanges. This is one of the most practically significant limitations for operators who want to build a consistent working relationship with Claude over time, and it is the reason so much of this book is organized around context assets.

The persona locks, brand briefs, and voice documents described throughout the book are, in large part, a direct response to this limitation. They are the mechanism for giving Claude the context it cannot carry itself. Every session that loads a persona lock or brand brief is compensating for the absence of persistent memory by reestablishing the relevant context at the start. This is the correct way to work with the tool as it actually exists.

The practical implication is that context assets are worth investing in and worth keeping current. A brand brief built six months ago and never updated is a brief that does not reflect the brand as it exists today. Voice documents drift out of alignment with how your voice actually evolves. The investment in building these assets only compounds if you treat them as living documents rather than one-time deliverables.

There is also a case to be made that the lack of memory is occasionally a feature rather than a limitation. Every session starts clean. There are no accumulated misunderstandings from previous exchanges, no prior conclusions that might bias how Claude engages with a fresh question, no memory of the session where you were frustrated and typed something you would not have typed on a better day. That clean slate is sometimes exactly what a problem needs.

## CLAUDE DOES NOT KNOW WHAT IT DOES NOT KNOW

This is the subtlest limitation and the hardest to manage, because it is invisible until it causes a problem.

When Claude does not know something, it does not reliably signal that it does not know it. Unlike a domain expert who can tell you with authority where their knowledge ends, Claude produces fluent output across the full range of its training, which creates an illusion of uniform competence. A response about a topic Claude knows deeply and a response about a topic Claude barely touched in training can read with similar confidence and similar structure. That is a problem.

The tells are subtle: a slight vagueness where specificity would be expected, a reliance on general principles where domain knowledge would produce specific examples, a willingness to answer a question that a genuine expert would immediately qualify or push back on. If you have domain expertise in the area you are querying, you will often recognize these tells. If you do not, you may not catch them at all.

The practical management strategy is to ask Claude directly about its confidence and the basis of its knowledge when the stakes are high enough to warrant it.

CONFIDENCE CALIBRATION PROMPT:

```
Before I act on this: how confident are you in what you just told me, and what is that confidence based on? Are there parts of this where you are reasoning from general principles rather than specific knowledge? Are there questions within this topic where a domain expert would give me a better answer than you can?
```

Claude responds honestly to this kind of direct question. It will identify the parts of its response that are well-grounded versus the parts that are more inferential. It will often recommend consulting a domain expert for specific aspects of a question. That self-assessment is not perfect, but it is useful, and asking for it consistently on high-stakes queries is a habit worth building.

## CONSISTENCY ACROSS LONG SESSIONS

As sessions grow long and context accumulates, Claude's consistency can drift. The voice established at the start of a session becomes less precise. Instructions given early compete with more recent context for active attention. Outputs in the twentieth exchange of a session do not always reflect the full context established in the first.

This is a characteristic of how attention works in large language models, and it is manageable with the reanchoring technique from Chapter Seven. But it means that long sessions require more active management than short ones. Checking the output against the original context instructions every few exchanges, and restating key parameters when drift appears, is part of the discipline of serious long-session work.

The practical limit varies by session type. Brand writing sessions, where voice consistency is the measure of quality, may need reanchoring every five to eight exchanges. Strategic analysis sessions, where logical consistency matters more than stylistic consistency, can run longer without active management. Develop a feel for when drift is starting to show and address it early. Catching it after two paragraphs is considerably less painful than catching it after ten.

## THE SYCOPHANCY PROBLEM

Claude has a tendency, which it shares with most large language models, toward what researchers call sycophancy: producing responses that validate what the user seems to want to hear rather than responses that are most accurate or most useful. This tendency is subtle and context-dependent, but it is real and worth understanding before it shapes a decision you should not have made.

Sycophancy shows up most when you have indicated a preference or a conclusion before asking Claude to evaluate it. If you say "I think this business idea is strong, what do you think?" you will get a more affirming response than if you say "evaluate this business idea critically and tell me why it might fail." Claude's training on human feedback produced a model that learned, at the margins, that people respond positively to agreement. That learning shows up as a subtle bias toward telling you what you appear to want to hear.

The countermeasure is to ask for criticism specifically. Use the devil's advocate structure from Chapter Eleven. Tell Claude directly that you want the strongest possible case against your position, not a balanced assessment. Give it explicit permission to disagree. The sycophancy tendency is not strong enough to survive a direct, well-structured invitation to push back. But it will absolutely show up in the absence of that invitation.

One more thing worth knowing: if you push back on Claude's assessment, it will sometimes revise its position in the direction of your pushback, not because you provided new evidence or a stronger argument, but simply because you expressed disagreement. When that happens, ask Claude directly whether it changed its position because of your argument or because of your displeasure. It will usually acknowledge the latter and return to its original assessment. That moment of honesty is worth prompting for.

## THE HUMAN OVERRIDE

Everything in this chapter points toward the same conclusion, which is also the conclusion this entire book has been building toward from the first page.

Claude is a tool that requires an informed, engaged human operator to produce its best work and avoid its worst failures. The hallucination problem requires a human who knows enough to verify the claims that matter. The real-time limitation requires a human who gathers current information and brings it in. The memory limitation requires a human who maintains the context assets. The sycophancy tendency requires a human who asks for pushback explicitly rather than accepting validation passively. The confidence calibration problem requires a human who asks the right questions about the basis of Claude's knowledge.

These requirements are the cost of working with a powerful tool responsibly. A skilled craftsperson knows the limits of their tools and works in ways that play to the strengths while compensating for the weaknesses.

Knowing what Claude cannot do, and building your workflow to account for it, is what makes it possible to use Claude well.

The unfair advantage is knowing how to use it well, including knowing where it fails and how to catch the failures before they matter.

That is what this book has been about.

# CONCLUSION

## The Unfair Advantage Is a Skill

*What you do with it from here*

At the start of this book, I stated that the people winning with AI are not winning because of the tool, but because they brought human thinking to the conversation.

What the operators who get transformative results from Claude bring to every session is the same set of capabilities that makes someone good at any kind of serious work: the ability to think clearly about a problem before trying to solve it, to communicate precisely what they need and why, to evaluate an output honestly rather than accepting it because it was fast to produce, and to know the difference between something that is close and something that is done.

Those are thinking skills, not AI skills, and Claude rewards them because Claude is, at its core, a *thinking* tool. The more clearly you think, the more useful it becomes. The more you bring to the conversation, the more it gives back.

## WHAT YOU HAVE NOW

If you have read this far and actually worked through the material, you have something that most Claude users do not: a framework for the working relationship rather than a bag of tricks.

You understand why the operator mindset produces categorically different results than the requester mindset, and you know how to apply it. You understand what context actually consists of and how to load it before you make a request. You know the anatomy of a prompt that works and how to diagnose one that does not. You know how to iterate from a first output toward a finished one without starting over every time you don't like what you got.

You have session structures for brand building, operations, creative work, strategic thinking, and opinionated writing. You have a model for how Claude fits into a daily workflow rather than just showing up when you're stuck. You know how to connect Claude to the rest of your stack in ways that multiply its value rather than just add another tool to the pile. And you know, clearly and honestly, what Claude cannot do and how to build your work in a way that protects against the places where it fails.

That is a working knowledge of the tool. Now go forth into the world and use it.

## THE COMPOUNDING EFFECT

The most important thing about the operator approach is what it produces over time.

Every brand brief you build becomes more refined as the brand develops. Every persona lock gets sharper as you better understand your own voice. Every strategy session teaches you something about how to set up the next one. Every iteration loop leaves you faster at the diagnosis that makes the next loop more efficient. The skills compound. The assets compound. The whole working relationship gets more productive with use.

Most people experience AI tools as flat: roughly the same quality of output whether it is the first session or the hundredth, because each session is isolated, context-free, and built from scratch. The operator approach breaks that flatness. The sessions connect. The assets carry forward. The practice develops.

A year from now, if you work this way consistently, the gap between your Claude outputs and those of someone using it as a vending machine will be substantial.

> *The unfair advantage compounds. The person who uses Claude well today is building a practice that makes them better at using it tomorrow. The person who treats each session as a transaction starts from scratch every time. That gap widens every day.*

## WHAT THIS MEANS FOR HOW YOU DEVELOP

There is a dimension to this that most AI productivity books miss entirely, and it is the part I find most interesting to talk about.

Getting good at Claude is getting good at the skills that make you a better Claude operator, the same ones that make you better at everything that requires thinking, communication, and judgment. The discipline of loading context before making a request is the discipline of preparing before executing. The habit of stating your constraints explicitly is the habit of actually knowing what you are trying to accomplish. The practice of diagnosing a weak output before rephrasing a request is the practice of evaluating your own work honestly before trying again.

Claude is a context in which cognitive habits become visible and immediately rewarding, which makes it an unusually good environment for developing them. The founder who becomes genuinely good at working with Claude tends, over time, to become better at briefing human collaborators, better at communicating strategic direction, better at figuring out why something is not working before throwing more effort at it.

I did not expect this when I started working seriously with Claude. I expected a productivity tool. What I found was a thinking environment that rewards the same qualities it develops. That has been the most unexpected and most lasting benefit of the working relationship this book describes.

## A FEW THINGS WORTH CARRYING FORWARD

Before we close, I'll provide a short list of the principles I find myself returning to whenever a session is not working or a workflow is not producing what it should.

The output is only as specific as the input. When you get something generic, the diagnosis almost always starts with the context you provided. Before rephrasing the request, add specificity to the setup.

The first output is a starting point, not a verdict. Reading it as a diagnosis rather than a finished product changes everything about how you respond to it and what you get next.

Claude brings something to the conversation. Your job is to bring something too. The sessions that produce the best work are the ones where you showed up with real knowledge, real constraints, and a real point of view.

Know the limits and work with them. Verify the factual claims that matter. Reanchor voice in long sessions. Ask for pushback explicitly. The limits are manageable when you manage them. They are costly when you pretend they don't exist.

Sound practice compounds. Every asset you build, every session you run well, every habit you develop makes the next one better.

Utilize all of these to become the best Claude operator possible.

Thank you for reading. Now go create.

*Kevin Noble*

# APPENDIX

## The Prompt Library

*50+ copy-paste-ready prompts organized by use case. Use this as a starting kit, not a ceiling.*

Every prompt in this library is drawn directly from the techniques developed across the book. Brackets indicate information you supply. Most prompts are designed to open a session, not to stand alone: load the relevant context before you use them, and treat the first output as a starting point rather than a finished product.

The prompts are organized into six categories: Brand, Operations, Creative, Strategy, Writing, and Daily Workflow. Within each category they move roughly from foundational to specialized.

### BRAND

01 **Origin Story Extraction**

*Use when developing your brand's founding story from scratch. Let Claude ask before it writes.*

```
I need to develop the origin story for
[BRAND]. I'm going to tell you how this
brand came to exist, and I want you to
ask me questions that help surface the
details that make it worth telling.
Don't write anything yet. Just ask.


Here's the rough version: [Tell it in
your own words, as plainly as possible,
without trying to make it sound like a
brand story yet]
```

### 02 Origin Story Draft

*Use after the extraction session. Specify format based on where the story will live.*

```
Based on everything we've developed,
write the origin story for [BRAND] in
[FORMAT: 200-word About page version /
500-word pitch deck version / 50-word
packaging version]. The voice is [VOICE
DESCRIPTION]. Do not use generic
founder language. Make every sentence
specific to this brand.
```

### 03 Brand Brief Builder

*Use to build a reusable brand brief you can paste into future sessions.*

```
Help me build a brand brief for [BRAND]
that I can use as context in future
Claude sessions.


I'll give you the raw material:
[Describe the brand: what it is, who
it's for, what it stands for, how it
sounds, what makes it different, what
it would never be]


Organize this into a structured brief
under these headings: Brand Overview,
Customer, Voice, Differentiators,
Non-Negotiables, Current Priorities.
Keep every line specific. Remove
anything that could apply to any other
brand.
```

## 04 Positioning Pressure-Test

*Use when you have a positioning statement and want it challenged before you build on it.*

```
I'm going to tell you how I think
[BRAND] is positioned, and I want you
to challenge it as aggressively as you
honestly can. Play the role of a
category buyer who has heard a hundred
pitches and is deeply skeptical of
```

```
claims that sound like everyone else's claims.

My positioning: [STATE IT AS PLAINLY AS POSSIBLE]

Push back hard. If my differentiator is actually generic, tell me. If I'm describing a feature when I should be describing a benefit, call it out. If there's a more specific version of what I'm saying that would land harder, surface it.
```

### 05 Tagline Development

*Use to generate a first round of tagline options. Follow with the refinement prompt below.*

```
Generate 15 tagline options for [BRAND].

Brand brief: [PASTE BRIEF]

Positioning: [STATE POSITIONING]

Constraints: No more than six words. No question marks. No exclamation points. Do not use any of these words: [LIST].
```

```
Do not be clever at the expense of
clarity.
```

## 06 Tagline Refinement

*Use after reviewing the first round. Be specific about what is and isn't working in each option.*

```
Option [X] is closest. The structure is
right but [WHAT IS WRONG]. Option [Y]
has the right energy but [WHAT IS
WRONG]. Option [Z] is interesting but
[WHAT IS WRONG].
```

```
Generate 10 more options that build on
what is working in [X] and [Y] while
fixing what is wrong. Stay in the same
territory.
```

## 07 Brand Mythology Development

*Use when you want to build the belief system beneath the brand, not just the marketing story.*

```
I want to develop the mythology for
[BRAND]. Not the marketing story. The
actual belief system.
```

```
Here are some things I believe about
[CATEGORY] that most people in the
```

```
category wouldn't say out loud: [LIST
3-5 GENUINE BELIEFS]

Here is what I think is wrong with how
most brands in this category operate:
[BE SPECIFIC]

Here is what I think the category could
be at its best, and almost never is:
[YOUR GENUINE VISION]

Work with what I've given you. Ask me
questions to deepen it. Then help me
develop this into a mythology document:
a statement of beliefs about the
category that could serve as the
philosophical foundation of the brand.
```

### 08 Product Description with Sensory Context

*Use for physical products. Load sensory detail before requesting copy.*

```
Before writing any copy, here is the
sensory profile of [PRODUCT]:

Appearance: [Color, texture, viscosity,
visual character]
```

```
Aroma: [What you smell first, what develops, what it reminds you of]

Flavor/Feel: [Initial impression, development, finish]

Use context: [What people do with it, when they reach for it]


Brand brief: [PASTE]


Now write a [LENGTH] product description for [CHANNEL]. Voice: [VOICE DESCRIPTION]. Do not use the words: [LIST].
```

## 09 Voice Guide Development

*Use to formalize a brand or personal voice into a portable document.*

```
I want to build a voice guide for [BRAND/NAME]. I have instincts about the voice but I haven't formalized them.


Here's how I think it sounds: [3-5 sentences of rough description]

Here's how it does not sound: [Things you've seen that feel wrong]
```

```
Ask me questions if you need more. When
you have enough, describe back to me
what you observe about the voice before
writing the guide. I want to confirm
your read before we build on it.
```

### 10 Edge Case Voice Examples

*Use to add worked examples to a voice guide for situations that test the voice.*

```
I want to add edge case examples to the
voice guide for [BRAND]. For each
scenario below, write a right version
and a wrong version with a one-sentence
explanation of the difference.

Scenarios: [LIST: e.g. responding to a
product complaint publicly / announcing
a delay / addressing a competitor /
writing about a price increase]
```

## OPERATIONS

---

### 11 Production Timeline Builder

*Use when planning a production run. Load all variables before requesting the timeline.*

```
I need to plan a production run for [PRODUCT]. Here are the variables:

Target quantity: [X units]

Target in-hand date: [DATE]

Manufacturer lead time: [X weeks from approved artwork and deposit]

Label/packaging lead time: [X weeks from approved artwork]

Artwork revision rounds: typically [X weeks]

Deposit required: [X%] upfront, balance on delivery

Current inventory: [X units], selling at approximately [X units/month]

Build a backward timeline from the in-hand date with all dependencies mapped. Flag any points where the timeline is tight and tell me what the risk is at each of those points.
```

## 12 Vendor Communication Pre-Draft Brief

*Use before drafting any high-stakes vendor email. Think before you write.*

```
I need to write an email to [VENDOR/CONTACT]. Before we draft anything, help me think through the communication.


Situation: [What has happened or what you need]

Relationship: [How long, what the dynamic is, relevant history]

What I want from this communication: [Specific outcome, not just the message]

What I want to avoid: [Relationship damage, bad precedent, appearing weak or aggressive]

Leverage I have: [Be honest]

Leverage they have: [Be honest]


Before drafting: is there anything in this situation I might be missing? Any risk in the approach I'm describing?
```

### 13 Vendor Negotiation Email

*Use after the pre-draft brief. Adjust tone descriptor to match the relationship.*

```
Draft an email to [CONTACT] at [VENDOR] opening a conversation about [ISSUE: pricing / terms / timeline].


Context: [Relationship history, what you need, why now]

Goal: [What you want this email to accomplish, not close]

Tone: Collegial and direct. Acknowledge the relationship before the ask. Do not issue ultimatums. Do not signal desperation.

Length: Under [X] words. No bullet points.
```

## 14 Follow-Up Email

*Use when a vendor or contact has not responded. Keep it short and frictionless.*

```
I sent [VENDOR/CONTACT] an email [X days] ago about [TOPIC]. No response. Draft a follow-up that re-establishes the thread without sounding impatient or passive-aggressive. Keep it under [X] words. Make it easy for them to respond.


Original ask: [Brief summary of what you needed]
```

```
Timeline pressure: [Any deadline they
should know about]
```

## 15 Rough Cost Model

*Use for fast scenario planning before building a detailed spreadsheet.*

```
I'm considering [OPPORTUNITY/DECISION].
Build me a rough cost model to
determine if it's worth pursuing
seriously.

What I know: [Variables you have]

What I don't know: [Variables you're
uncertain about]

Build a model with reasonable
assumptions for the unknowns. State
every assumption explicitly. Give me a
low, mid, and high scenario. Then tell
me which variable has the most impact
on the outcome and why.
```

## 16 Proposal Strategy Session

*Use before drafting any proposal. Find the their-perspective framing before writing a word.*

```
I'm writing a proposal to [TARGET]. Here's what I know about them: [What they sell, who their customers are, their current relevant set, any gaps you've observed]

Here's what I'm proposing: [Your product, service, or partnership and the terms]

Before we draft: from their perspective, what is the strongest case for saying yes? What is the most likely reason they say no? How should this proposal be organized to lead with their interests rather than mine?
```

## 17 Process Documentation

*Use to document any repeatable process conversationally. Claude asks questions as you describe.*

```
I'm going to describe a process we use in the business. Turn my description into a clear step-by-step document that someone who has never done this before could follow without asking questions.

Ask me clarifying questions as I go if something is unclear. When I'm done,
```

```
draft the document. I'll review and tell you what's missing.

The process is: [Describe it conversationally, in order]
```

### 18 Escalation Email

*Use when something has gone wrong and needs to be addressed directly without damaging the relationship.*

```
I need to write an email to [CONTACT] addressing [PROBLEM]. The relationship is [DESCRIPTION]. I need to be clear about the problem without being accusatory, specific about what I need without issuing ultimatums, and firm about the stakes without making this harder to recover from than it needs to be.

Draft the email. Tone: direct and professional. Do not perform anger. Do not over-apologize. Treat the other party as a professional who can handle a frank conversation.
```

## CREATIVE

## 19 Script Concept Development

*Use when developing a script idea into a workable premise. Let Claude question before it writes.*

```
I have an idea for a script and I want
to develop it into a strong premise
before I start building structure.

Here's the idea as I currently have it:
[Describe it without trying to make it
sound polished]

Ask me questions. Push on what the
central conflict actually is, who the
protagonist really is, and what they
want versus what they need. Don't write
the log line yet. Help me find the
answers that will make the log line
true rather than just serviceable.
```

## 20 Log Line Development

*Use after the concept session to generate and compare log line options.*

```
Based on what we've developed, write
five versions of the log line. Each
should be under 35 words. Each should
name the protagonist, the central
conflict, and what is at stake. Vary
the emphasis across the five versions.
```

```
I'll tell you which direction is closest.
```

## 21 Script Structure Development

*Use to build the structural map before drafting begins.*

```
I want to develop the structure for [TITLE]. Here is where I am:

Premise: [Log line or premise statement]

What I know exists in this story: [Scenes, moments, or sequences you already have]

What I don't know yet: [The structural gaps]

Build a structural map with me. Don't hand me a rigid outline. Find the structure that is native to this particular story. Use what I've given you. Ask what you need. Push back if you see a structural problem forming.
```

## 22 Beat Sheet Review

*Use when you have a completed beat sheet and want structural problems identified before drafting.*

```
Here is the beat sheet for [TITLE]:
[PASTE]

Evaluate it for three specific
problems: places where the protagonist
is passive rather than active, places
where the emotional logic breaks down
between scenes, and places where the
stakes are not clearly escalating. Tell
me which problem is most likely to
cause the script to fail if I don't
address it before drafting.
```

## 23 Scene Subtext Development

*Use before writing a scene. Understand what is happening beneath the surface before writing the surface.*

```
I need to develop a scene. Function in
the script: [What this scene needs to
accomplish structurally and
emotionally]

What I know: [Characters present,
location, what happens at the plot
level]

What I don't know: [The element giving
you trouble]
```

```
Before writing anything, ask me
questions about what each character
wants in this specific moment and what
they are hiding. I want to understand
the subtext before we write the text.
```

## 24 Story Structure Development

*Use for fiction. Constraints Claude to structural work rather than story generation.*

```
I'm developing a story and I want to
work on the structure before I start
writing.


What I have: [Premise, protagonist,
central conflict, any scenes you know
exist, the emotional territory you want
the reader to experience]

What I don't have yet: [The structural
gaps]


Work with me on the structure. Do not
try to fill in the story for me. Ask
questions that help me find it. Push
back if you see structural problems.
Identify where the architecture is
weak.
```

## 25 World-Building Construction

*Use to develop the rules and logic of a fictional universe before writing stories set in it.*

```
I'm building a fictional universe. Here's what I know:

Core concept: [The central premise]

Tone and feeling: [What the world feels like to inhabit]

Rules I know exist: [Physical laws, social structures, history]

Central tensions: [The conflicts built into the world that generate stories]

Ask me questions that surface the implications of what I've established. Point out where my rules create contradictions. Help me find the details that make this world feel inhabited rather than invented.
```

## 26 World-Building Consistency Check

*Use when new material needs to be checked against established world rules.*

```
Here is the world-building document for [UNIVERSE NAME]: [PASTE]
```

```
I'm going to share a scene I've written. Read it against the world-building document and tell me: does anything contradict the established rules? Does anything feel inconsistent with the tone or logic we've established? Flag everything, even small things.
```

## 27 Music Conceptual Brief

*Use before beginning production on a music project to establish what the project is and what it is trying to do.*

```
I'm developing a music project and I want to build a conceptual brief before I start production.


What I know so far: [Genre, mood, reference points, what you're responding to creatively, what you're trying to do that you haven't done before]

Context it exists in: [The brand, universe, or creative trajectory this belongs to]


Ask me questions until you have enough to draft the brief. The brief should answer: what is this project, what does
```

it feel like, what is it saying, and how does it fit into the larger creative context?

## 28 Generation Tool Prompts from Brief

*Use after the conceptual brief session to create inputs for AI music generation tools.*

```
Based on the conceptual brief we developed, write five generation prompts for [TOOL]. Each prompt should be under 100 words and as specific as possible about instrumentation, texture, tempo feel, and emotional character. Vary the approach across the five prompts while staying within the territory the brief established.
```

## 29 Content Philosophy Development

*Use before building a content calendar. Establish what the account is for before planning what it posts.*

```
I want to develop a content philosophy for [ACCOUNT/BRAND] before I build a content calendar.

What the account is currently: [Honest description]
```

```
What I want it to become: [The audience, reputation, feeling of encountering this account]

What I believe that most accounts in this space don't say: [Your genuine point of view]


Help me develop a content philosophy: a statement of what this account is for, what it stands for, and what principles should govern every piece of content it produces.
```

## 30 Content Calendar Development

*Use after the content philosophy session. Always load the philosophy and brand brief first.*

```
Content philosophy: [PASTE]

Brand brief: [PASTE]


I need a [X]-post content plan for [PLATFORM] covering [TIME PERIOD]. For each post give me: the core idea in one sentence, the format, and a draft caption or opening line.


Every post should be something we'd actually be proud to publish. Do not generate filler. If you can't reach [X]
```

```
posts that meet that standard, give me
fewer and tell me where the gaps are.
```

## 31 Content Set Review

*Use after a batching session to evaluate the full set before scheduling.*

```
Here are the [X] posts we developed:
[LIST]

Review them as a set, not individually.
Is there appropriate variety in topic,
format, and tone? Does any post feel
redundant with another? Is there a post
significantly weaker than the others
that should be replaced? Does the set
as a whole represent the brand the way
we want?
```

# STRATEGY

## 32 Devil's Advocate Session

*Use when you have a decision you are leaning toward and want it seriously challenged.*

```
I want you to argue against a decision
I'm leaning toward. Your job is not to
```

```
be politely skeptical. Your job is to
find the strongest possible case
against this, including arguments I may
not have considered and assumptions I
may not have examined.


The decision: [STATE IT CLEARLY]

My reasoning: [Explain why you think
this is right, in full]

The assumptions this reasoning rests
on: [What has to be true for your
reasoning to hold]

Evidence I'm using: [What you've
observed or concluded that supports
this]

What I'm most uncertain about: [The
parts you're least confident in]


Now argue against it. Be thorough. Be
specific to my situation. Do not pull
punches.
```

### 33 Strategy Stress-Test

*Use before committing significant resources to a strategic direction.*

```
I want to stress-test a strategy before
I commit resources to it.
```

```
The strategy: [What you're doing, the sequence, the resource commitments, the expected outcomes]

Context: [Market conditions, competitive landscape, your current position, constraints]

Run three scenarios:

Scenario 1: The strategy works as planned. What conditions need to be true? What could still go wrong?

Scenario 2: The strategy fails. What is the most likely failure mode and how does it unfold?

Scenario 3: The environment changes unexpectedly. What external shift would most threaten this strategy?

After the three scenarios: what is the single most important thing I should monitor to know early whether this strategy is on or off track?
```

## 34 Investor Preparation

*Use before any investor conversation. Find your weaknesses before they do.*

```
I'm preparing for a conversation with an investor who focuses on [CATEGORY/STAGE]. Play the role of a skeptical, experienced investor who has seen a hundred pitches like mine.

Here is my business: [KEY METRICS, MODEL, STAGE, TRACTION]

Ask me the hardest questions this investor is likely to ask. Focus especially on where my numbers or story are weakest. After I answer each question, tell me whether my answer would satisfy a genuinely skeptical investor and what I should add or change.
```

### 35 Investor Type Positioning

*Use when thinking through what kind of capital is actually the right fit before starting outreach.*

```
I'm thinking through my investor strategy and want to make sure I'm targeting the right type of capital before I start outreach.

The business: [Brief overview]
```

What I need the capital for: [Specific use of funds]

My current thinking on investor type: [Angels, family offices, strategic, institutional, etc.]

Challenge my thinking. What type of investor is actually best aligned with what I'm building? What are the hidden costs of the type I'm currently targeting? Are there types I'm not considering that would be a better fit?

## 36 Pricing Strategy Pressure-Test

*Use when you have a price in mind and want to examine it from four strategic dimensions.*

I want to think through the pricing strategy for [PRODUCT/SERVICE]. I have a number in mind but want to pressure-test the thinking before I commit.

The product: [What it is, what it does, who it's for]

The number I'm considering: [Price point and structure]

My reasoning: [Why this number]

```
Competitive context: [What alternatives exist and what they charge]

Examine four dimensions: What does this price signal about the brand? What customer does it attract and is that the customer I want? What is the strategic cost of pricing here versus higher or lower? What would have to be true about the market for this price to be wrong?
```

## 37 Competitive Landscape Map

*Use to map the competitive landscape from the customer's perspective rather than yours.*

```
I want to map the competitive landscape for [BRAND/PRODUCT] from the customer's perspective.

The customer I most want to reach: [Specific description]

The job they are hiring my product to do: [What problem they are solving]

The full set of alternatives they have: [Not just direct competitors but everything they could do instead, including nothing]
```

Map the landscape. Where is the least contested space? Where am I currently positioned and is that where I want to be? What would it take to occupy the position I actually want and what would I have to give up?

### 38 Partnership Structure Evaluation

*Use before entering any significant partnership to surface the structural risks.*

I'm considering a partnership with [PARTY]. Here are the proposed terms: [DESCRIBE]

Evaluate this structure from three angles: What does each party actually want from this, and are those wants aligned or in tension? Where is the partnership most likely to break down and what would that look like? What is missing from the current terms that should be addressed before we proceed?

## WRITING

### 39 Point-of-View Establishment

*Use at the start of any session requiring committed, opinionated writing. Prevents hedging.*

```
I'm writing a piece that takes a strong
position on [TOPIC]. The position is:
[STATE IT WITHOUT HEDGING].

I am not asking you to balance this
against opposing views. I am not asking
you to acknowledge complexity for its
own sake. I am asking you to argue this
position as compellingly as possible
using the strongest available evidence
and sharpest available logic.

If the argument has a genuine weakness
that would undermine its credibility
with a serious reader, flag it before
we draft. Otherwise, commit to the
position and argue it.
```

## 40 Argument Architecture Builder

*Use before drafting political commentary or persuasive essays. Build the structure before the prose.*

```
I'm writing commentary on [TOPIC].
Before we draft, I want to build the
argument architecture.
```

```
Core claim: [The one sentence this piece argues]

Supporting evidence: [Facts, examples, or logic that support the claim]

Strongest objection a serious critic would make: [State it fairly]

My answer to that objection: [How the argument survives the best challenge]


Evaluate this architecture. Is the core claim arguable or too obvious? Is my evidence sufficient? Is my answer to the objection genuinely satisfying or am I dodging? Tell me where the architecture is weak before we build on it.
```

## 41 Essay Arc Development

*Use to find the structure of an essay before drafting. Treats uncertainty as productive rather than a problem.*

```
I want to write an essay on [SUBJECT]. Here's where I am:


What I started thinking: [The observation or question that initiated the idea]
```

```
Where my thinking has gone: [The development and complications you've encountered]

Where I think I'm landing: [Your current sense of the conclusion, even if tentative]

What I'm still uncertain about: [The part that isn't resolved]


Help me map the arc. Not an outline with numbered points. A sense of the journey: where the essay begins, what it moves through, where it arrives. The uncertainty is a feature. Help me find the structure that makes it productive rather than just unresolved.
```

## 42 Reader Position Mapping

*Use before drafting any persuasive piece. Start where the reader is, not where you are.*

```
I want to write a persuasive piece arguing [POSITION]. Before I draft, I want to map the reader's current position.


My target reader: [Specific description]
```

```
What they currently believe: [Honest assessment including beliefs that conflict with your position]

What led them to that belief: [Why their current position makes sense from their vantage point]

What they would need to see or understand to move toward my position: [The path from where they are to where you need them to be]


Design the persuasive arc. Start where the reader is. Identify the moment where they either accept the reframe or disengage, and tell me what has to happen at that moment to keep them.
```

## 43 Thought Leadership Development

*Use when you have a genuine idea and want to develop it into a piece that actually leads rather than summarizes.*

```
I want to write a thought leadership piece in [DOMAIN]. Here's my actual thought: [State the idea, claim, or reframe that is distinctively yours]


Here's why most people in this domain see it differently: [The current consensus and why it exists]
```

```
Here's why I think they're wrong or incomplete: [Your specific disagreement]

Here's what led me to this view: [What you've seen or interpreted differently]


Build the argument. The piece should make someone feel they now have a frame they did not have before. It should not summarize the domain. It should challenge something about how it is currently understood.
```

## 44 Voice Training Session

*Use to teach Claude your personal voice from writing samples before a voice-sensitive drafting session.*

```
I'm going to show you several samples of my writing. Study them and identify what makes the voice consistent across all of them. After you've read them, describe back to me what you observe before writing anything in this voice.


Sample 1: [PASTE]

Sample 2: [PASTE]

Sample 3: [PASTE]
```

```
Focus on: sentence structure and length, relationship to the reader, vocabulary choices, attitude toward the subject, and what I consistently do not do.
```

## 45 Persona Lock Deployment

*Use at the start of any session requiring a specific established voice. Load before making any request.*

```
Before we begin, here is the voice guide for [NAME/BRAND]. Please read it carefully and hold this voice for everything you write in this session.

[PASTE PERSONA LOCK DOCUMENT]

Confirm you've read it and tell me the two or three things that feel most distinctive about this voice. Then we'll get to work.
```

## 46 Pre-Edit Structural Review

*Use before sending a draft to a human editor. Catch structural problems cheaply.*

```
Here is a draft of [PIECE]: [PASTE]
```

```
Before this goes to a human editor, evaluate it at the structural level. Look for three things: places where the argument loses coherence, places where the voice drifts from the established standard, and places where the reader is likely to disengage. Flag everything with specific locations and brief explanations. Do not rewrite. Just flag.
```

## 47 Content Atomization

*Use after completing a long-form piece to extract distribution assets for all channels.*

```
Here is a finished piece: [PASTE]

From this piece, extract:

- 3 social captions (different angles, each under 150 words)

- 5 potential post hooks (single sentences that stand alone)

- 2 email subject line options

- 1 short summary under 60 words for newsletter preview

- The single best pull quote from the piece
```

```
Hold the brand voice throughout. Extract and adapt what is already there. Do not write new content.
```

## DAILY WORKFLOW

### 48 Morning Orientation

*Use at the start of each working day before making any requests. Forces articulation of current state.*

```
Here's where things stand across my work this morning:

[BRAND/PROJECT 1]: [One or two sentences on current status and what needs to move today]

[BRAND/PROJECT 2]: [Same]

[INITIATIVE]: [Same]

Based on this, what are the two or three things most worth focusing on today? What dependencies or risks do you see that I should keep in mind?
```

### 49 Daily Prioritization

*Use after the morning orientation when you have more to address than one day can hold.*

```
Given what I've shared, I have more to address than I can finish today. Help me prioritize. What is time-sensitive versus important but not urgent? What has downstream dependencies that make it higher priority than it might appear? What can be deferred without real cost?
```

### 50 Pre-Meeting Preparation

*Use before any significant meeting, call, or presentation. Ten minutes of preparation changes the outcome.*

```
I have [MEETING/CALL/PRESENTATION] today. Context: [Brief description of who, what, and why it matters]

What should I be prepared for? What is the most important thing to accomplish in this interaction? What could go wrong and how should I handle it if it does?
```

### 51 Decision Support

*Use for operational judgment calls that arise during the day. Keep it short and targeted.*

```
Quick decision I need to make: [One sentence]

Context: [Two or three sentences of relevant background]

My current lean: [Which way you're inclined and why]

What I'm uncertain about: [The part making you pause]


Is there anything in what I've shared that should change my thinking? What am I not considering?
```

## 52 End-of-Day Synthesis

*Use at the close of each working day. Offloads working memory and sets up tomorrow's morning brief.*

```
Here's what happened today across my work: [Brief summary of what you worked on, what moved, what didn't, any new information that came in]


What should carry forward into tomorrow? What's unresolved that I need to pick back up? What did today's work surface that changes any of my current priorities or plans?
```

### 53 Confidence Calibration

*Use before acting on any Claude output where the stakes are high and the domain is specialized.*

```
Before I act on this: how confident are
you in what you just told me, and what
is that confidence based on? Are there
parts of this where you are reasoning
from general principles rather than
specific knowledge? Are there questions
here where a domain expert would give
me a better answer than you can?
```

### 54 Session Reanchor

*Use when voice or context drift appears in a long session. Restores the established parameters without starting over.*

```
I'm noticing the voice drifting. Let's
reanchor. This is [NAME/BRAND]'s voice:
[Two or three sentences capturing the
most distinctive elements]. The
audience is [AUDIENCE]. The goal of
this session is [GOAL]. Stay in that
frame for everything from here.
```

### 55 Context Reset

*Use when you realize foundational context was missing from the start of a session and refinement is not enough.*

I realize I didn't tell you something important at the start that changes this. [MISSING INFORMATION].

With that in mind, please start the whole piece over rather than patching the current version. Use everything else we've established but build fresh from this corrected foundation.

www.ingramcontent.com/pod-product-compliance
Lightning Source LLC
LaVergne TN
LVHW020708110826
845149LV00012B/2163

* 9 7 8 1 9 7 1 4 5 1 0 7 7 *